CW01498014

GENERATION DRIFT

For Andy, Viv, Cali & Pickle

GENERATION DRIFT

WHY WE'RE UP CAREER CREEK
AND HOW TO PADDLE HOME

JOSH ROBERTS

Please note that topics such as depression and suicide are mentioned throughout the book. If you are struggling with your mental health please talk to a medical professional for advice.

First published in Great Britain in 2022 by Yellow Kite
An Imprint of Hodder & Stoughton
An Hachette UK company

1

Copyright © Josh Roberts 2022

The right of Josh Roberts to be identified as the Author of the Work has been asserted by him in accordance with the Copyright, Designs and Patents Act 1988.

Illustrations and cover design © Cali Mackrill at Malik and Mack

All rights reserved. No part of this publication may be reproduced, stored in a retrieval system, or transmitted, in any form or by any means without the prior written permission of the publisher, nor be otherwise circulated in any form of binding or cover other than that in which it is published and without a similar condition being imposed on the subsequent purchaser.

A CIP catalogue record for this title is available from the British Library

Hardback ISBN 978 1 529 37724 8
eBook ISBN 978 1 529 37725 5

Typeset in Garamond by Hewer Text UK Ltd, Edinburgh
Printed and bound in Great Britain by Clays Ltd, Elcograf S.p.A.

Hodder & Stoughton policy is to use papers that are natural, renewable and recyclable products and made from wood grown in sustainable forests. The logging and manufacturing processes are expected to conform to the environmental regulations of the country of origin.

Yellow Kite
Hodder & Stoughton Ltd
Carmelite House
50 Victoria Embankment
London EC4Y 0DZ

www.yellowkitebooks.co.uk

CONTENTS

WELCOME TO CAREER CREEK

FOUR YEARS AGO I had an epiphany in a graveyard.

OK, maybe that's a bit over the top. Perhaps 'realisation' would be a more accurate descriptor, and while there were indeed graves, the burial ground in question was the very pretty, extremely touristic surrounds of Highgate Cemetery in north London. Hardly a scene from *The Omen*, I'll admit.

I'd been persuaded to go by my best friend, Olly, and I should say that graveyards aren't normal venues for our 'mate dates'. But after a spate of more conventional meetings in pubs, cinemas and the curry houses of south London, we wanted something more original. Two ideas were mooted: cycling or the cemetery. And while wandering around graveyards might seem spooky, nothing is more haunting than men in Lycra. We booked our tickets and boarded the Tube.

As it happened, our day with the deceased turned out to be the best mate date on record. And not just because, after having not seen each other for a while, Olly and I had tons to chat and laugh about. But also because I discovered how fascinating, important and life-affirming it can be to learn about those who've passed away – their achievements, failures, fragilities and flaws; what made them great and what made them human.

It also reminded me of an old idea – I think from Freud – about funerals. Lots of people know this one, but it's the idea that we find funerals so sad, not because of who's died, but because, in dying, that person forces us to confront our own mortality. Seeing Steve or Susan in their wooden box, the theory goes, reminds us that one day we'll find ourselves in a similar spot, buried beneath six feet of London clay and a few wilted carnations.

It's a neat theory, but like much of Freud it's both clever and yet not quite right. It's not our mortality that we fear, it's not death itself that worries us; it's dying before we've achieved what we want to achieve. Or, worse still, it's dying before finding out what we want to achieve.

Which – and this was the epiphany/realisation – was exactly where I was. After 26 years on this earth, and despite trying really pretty hard, I still hadn't the foggiest what I should do with my life.

Actually, that's not totally true . . .

There were some spheres of my life where I knew *exactly* what I should do. Even then, I was certain, for example, that I'd found the girl – Cali – who I wanted to spend my life with. And I was also convinced that I wanted kids at some point. Plus, I wanted to learn the piano, and travel, and read lots of books, and get really good at bolognaise sauce (an Italian friend says the secret is lots of red wine), and get really good at sex (an Italian friend says the secret is lots of red wine).

So, when it came to the hobbies and extracurriculars, I was quite clear what I'd like to achieve over the next 40 years. The issue was work. Or, more specifically, the issue was not knowing what I could do, or be good at, or even enjoy. Instead, I was drifting through my 'career'. And, sadly, in feeling like this I wasn't alone.

> Versus our parents, millennials like me are twice as bored of their work and nearly three times as likely to leave their job. And that was before a coronavirus rocked up and started wreaking havoc, slashing jobs and destroying livelihoods.

The weird thing is that I don't think many of us saw it coming; not the pandemic, the unhappiness at work. Growing up in the nineties and early noughties, in the Union Jack optimism of those pre-Iraq Blair years, I think we thought it was going to be plain sailing. Why wouldn't it be? The government was spending more on education, education, education than any before it. The unemployment rate was falling. Company share prices (as measured by the FTSE 100) seemed on the up and up. Why wouldn't that continue through our teens, into our twenties and onwards through our lives? Why wouldn't we discover jobs that we enjoyed or that paid us a reasonable salary or – whisper it – both?

The answer, of course, is nuanced, complex and even controversial (and the whole next chapter is devoted to it). But, at the time, the plan seemed very simple. The adults had it all worked out. All we had to do was turn up at school, go to our lessons and do our revision. If we did that then we'd get good exam results. And if we got those then we'd get our dream job at a brilliant company, buy a nice house with a pretty garden, marry a Spice Girl and live happily ever after.

The problem was that – aside from the doctors, lawyers, architects and teachers – very few of us had any idea what that 'dream job' might be. So, instead, most of us just took the first one we got offered. It didn't matter that we'd never really been into recruitment, or hospitality, or retail, or accounting. And the actual role itself mattered even less. 'Trainee Merchandise Assistant', great! 'Graduate Campaign Analyst', you bet! 'Junior Sales Executive (Capital Markets)', yes please! Just as long as it was a job that paid us actual money. After all, there was a global financial crisis, so if someone offered you a gig, you took it and tried to get on with it. 'Stick with it for at least two years,' our parents told us. 'You don't want people to think you're flaky.'

But we *were* flaky. Flaky, and ennuied, and impatient. We wanted it all, now. And social media made that ambition feel realistic. Everyone else, it seemed, was having a terrific time making oodles of dosh with minimal effort. Why couldn't we? How come Mark Zuckerberg gets to wear a T-shirt to work? How come Kylie Jenner doesn't have to commute an hour each way? I bet Zoella doesn't have to do photocopying, or performance reviews, or circulate the meeting minutes; why should I?

On their own, jealousy, impatience and boredom aren't necessarily bad emotions. Jealousy can inspire us to action. Impatience, combined with a willingness to work, can bring success. Boredom – as my parents used to say on long car journeys – shows that you have an active mind. But when you *combine* jealousy, impatience and boredom, particularly within the stuffy confines of the 9 to 5, they make for a potent cocktail. In fact, it's so potent that it leads many of us to burn out or have mental breakdowns.

At least, that's what happened to me.

Until recently, my 'career' (if we're really going to call it that) was a confused and convoluted affair involving six jobs in five years, countless more applications and a string of failed side hustles. It's reminiscent of a child's painting in that, if you squint hard enough, you can just make out what I was aiming for. But it would take a particularly proud parent to identify the purpose or logic behind my professional choices.

I started at a big consulting firm. I was both nervous and excited to be offered the role. The interview process had been long and tricky. I'd had to borrow my brother's suit, and get the train to London, and spend a whole day answering questions like, 'What does leadership mean to you?' So I was thrilled when they called with the good news. Not even the fact that I was to be based in their Crawley office could dampen my spirits.

My official title was 'Associate Consultant' and my department was called 'Profitability and Cost Management'. This was a euphemistic attempt to conceal what we really did, which was fire people for money. Yep, that's right. Companies that didn't have the moral fibre to do it themselves used to call us in to fire their employees. If you've seen that George Clooney movie, *Up in the Air*, it was like a budget version of that.

At the start, my job was going from desk to desk to find the people on the spreadsheet. 'Gregg Johnson? Have you got a minute?' 'Susan Cassels? Could you come with me?' Then, after six months, I graduated to handing out the leaflets at the end of the sackings; 'Your new start', it said on the cover with a picture of a yacht sailing into a sunset.

As might be obvious, it was a wretched job and I despised every moment of it. And yet, I stayed with it for nearly two years. Why? In part, I hung around because I needed the money. Or at least, that's the excuse I told myself. 'In this economy you'd be mad to walk away from a stable job; this is the start of your future,' I'd say as I left my flat each morning. In reality, of course, I could have survived. In that sense, I was extremely lucky. I could have moved back home or sofa-surfed, got a job in a pub for a bit, re-strategised, applied for some other jobs.

The bigger problem was that doing so would have involved quitting a job which other people had wanted. And that, in truth, is what stopped me leaving. Plus, I didn't want people to think I was weak. I didn't want them to think I couldn't hack it. I wanted them to think I was tough, and hard-nosed, and hard-working. 'Here comes Josh,' I wanted them to say. 'Isn't he the high-flying consultant?' Pathetic, I know. But it's the truth.

It was an eight-week project in Luton which, finally, made me see the light. Two months living out of a suitcase in an airport Travelodge will do that. I just couldn't take it anymore. The misery of the firings, and the spreadsheets, and the fried breakfasts, and the uncomfortable shoes.

'What will you do next?' asked the Partner in my exit interview.

'I'm not sure,' I said. 'I'm really not sure.'

Storyteller Media was a young, cool advertising sales agency based in Covent Garden. There was a beer fridge, and a sound system, and everyone wore trainers. Which weren't the only reasons why I joined, but they *were* reasons. More important, however, was the fact that they offered fun and autonomy.

After two years of having no control over what I worked on, with whom and for whom, I wanted to be the master of my own destiny. Which is exactly what the Storyteller job (ostensibly flogging print advertising to unsuspecting marketers) gave me. It was meritocratic – the harder I worked, the more money I made. It didn't matter how long I'd been there, or whether the boss liked me. All that mattered was how much I tried. And that, along with the ping-pong and pub trips, appealed to me a great deal.

After 18 months, though, I grew bored. The hangovers seemed to get worse, so I stopped going to the pub. And the sales targets got harder, so the hour-long ping-pong sessions dried up, too. What remained was a very challenging and monotonous sales gig involving 100+ cold calls a day and lots of being told to 'fuck off'. I started sniffing around job sites and speaking to recruiters, and within a month or two found myself working at a bank.

I haven't a clue why. The money was good, I guess. Plus I had a fancy title: 'Senior Business Analyst – Marketing', which was curious given that I didn't spend any time analysing businesses. In fact, I didn't do anything at all. No one seemed to. The whole bank – with the exception of the folks in the branches – seemed to be one big exercise in time-wasting, ego, arse-covering and incompetence.

Which is to say nothing of the meetings. Oh, the meetings. God how I hated the meetings – the quantity of them, the quality of them, the fact that absolutely nothing would be decided at them. Except, of course, the need to have a follow-up one. 'Shall we take the action to circle back and touch base with a follow-up by close of play next week?' Sigh.

Most days were filled with a combination of online chess, perusing the easyJet sale and planning what to cook for dinner. And when BBC Good Food had run out of ideas, I took to booking meeting rooms to watch Netflix, and napping in the loos. You'd be surprised just how comfortable a travel pillow fashioned from spare loo rolls can be.

It was while working at the bank that things started to unravel for me.

You might think that, with so little to do professionally, I was able to enjoy a flourishing social life. But this was pre-pandemic – before working from home became a 'thing' – when being seen in the office was still considered essential. I had to be in before my boss and leave after him. There was no option but to sit there at my desk, mindlessly refreshing Microsoft Outlook, waiting for him to go home. Which meant that, despite having nothing to do, I was spending 80+ hours a week sitting in the office, bored to tears. Quite literally, by the way. After only a few months I took to crying in the loos. The first time it happened, it took me by surprise. But after a while it became part of my routine, just something I did in between pointless meetings.

Which is the pertinent word in all this – 'pointless'. Having so little to do, having so little responsibility or direction, rendered my life pointless. I could have stayed at home for weeks and no one would have noticed. And I found that painful, sad and, occasionally, infuriating. The anthropologist David Graeber called it 'a profound psychological violence', and he was right. 'How can one even begin to speak of dignity in labour,' he wrote in *Strike* magazine, 'when one secretly feels one's job should not exist?'

I should have quit, but I couldn't. I was trapped – by the money and the title. But also by the fear of the unknown and by my unwillingness to accept I'd made a bad decision (more on all this later). When I'd taken the job I'd been so sure that it was my future. I felt certain that I'd set the correct course and I'd bleated on to friends and family about my fantastic new job. Quitting ran counter to all that. To resign was to admit that I'd got it wrong. Worse, it meant confronting the fact that I hadn't a clue what I wanted to do with my life.

So, instead of quitting, I slogged it out for a year. And it was in the middle of that year that I had the mental breakdown. I've written elsewhere about this experience (and the subsequent one of living with an acute anxiety disorder), so I shan't bore you with it here. Suffice to say that it happened suddenly (the morning after a party), that it lasted for about two years and that it was uncompromisingly, unrelentingly bleak. It was 24 months of constant insomnia, worry and despair. I cried lots, slept little and thought often about killing myself.

I'm sure there were lots of reasons why I broke down, but work was unquestionably the biggest. 'Labor is the axis of human self-making,' said Gregory Baum. In my case, my work made my life dull, directionless and silly. As the boredom washed over me, as the once-vibrant colours of my life faded to beige, I felt hollow and lost. I questioned why I'd bothered. I lost interest in the things that used to bring me joy and pleasure. I grew tired and worn. I became negative, and grouchy, and withdrawn, and overweight.

It took things getting that bad for me to leave the bank. To do so, I devised a plan. In the immediate term I decided I needed a new job, fast. So I started ringing around my former Storyteller colleagues to see if anything was going.

Thankfully, there was. A different newspaper was on the hunt for an advertising sales wallah, and I grasped it with both hands. It was only ever a stopgap, but my goodness was it a welcome one.

Having escaped the hell of the bank, the next phase of the plan was to discover what I really might want to do. A year of soul-searching followed during which I kissed a wide variety of career frogs, including launching an impressive array of (now failed) 'side hustles'. There was my plan to sell falafel from a van, or my tech start-up to do with sales, or my ice cream boat idea. Actually, I stand by 'The Ice Lolly Rodger' – one day, I'm sure that'll be a monster hit.

Alongside the side hustles were at least 50 job applications and a smattering of subsequent interviews. At one stage I even dabbled with a career in reality TV. Yes, I know. You knew you recognised me from somewhere. *MasterChef UK*, series 15, episode 2 (and episode 2 only). Don't worry, I get it all the time. Don't crowd me please. No photos. I'm not doing selfies today.

Throughout all this, however, at the back of my mind was the idea that I might make a career from writing. Not in an irritating, Hollywood, 'you should quit your job and become a creative' sort of way. I'm not Dawn in *The Office*. I just thought it would be fun and stimulating and, having gone through my breakdown, I felt as though I might have something to talk about. I also knew that it would involve a monster pay cut, that I'd probably have to juggle a variety of weird and wacky income streams to make it happen and that there'd be a ton of rejection and lots of bemused conversations with my friends and family. And, perhaps unsurprisingly for a man with an anxiety disorder, I spent lots of time worrying about all of this – about money, and status, and how embarrassing it would be to get nowhere and have to crawl back to an office job, T.M.Lewin tie in hand. And, anyway, hadn't I left it too late? Hadn't people made up their minds by 28? Wasn't switching lanes completely impossible?

As you might have guessed, the answer to all of these questions has turned out to be no.

Which isn't to say that my fears were unfounded. Changing careers from salaried employment to writing a bit, talking a bit and doing part-time stuff a bit hasn't all been smooth sailing. It's demanded compromise and flexibility. And the pay cut, as I predicted, has been, well, put it this way, I know more about microwaving lentils than I could ever have imagined.

But I'm also no longer suicidal. I look forward to waking up. I get itchy on a Sunday knowing what awaits me on Monday. I enjoy what I do. Not always, but lots of the time. Most days I'm excited to sit down and do what I get paid for. And I'm convinced that you can be, too.

Which is what this book is all about.

The plan is simple. We'll begin by exploring why work doesn't seem to be working for so many of us millennials or Gen Zers (or whatever the newspapers are currently calling people under 40). We'll examine the myriad reasons why we're so uncertain, unfulfilled and unhappy with our careers. And, from this, we'll work out why so many folks my age and younger are drifting. Then, by combining my experiences with the thoughts of psychologists, academics and CEOs, we'll see what we can do about it.

And the good news is that there is loads of stuff that we can do about it. Even better, the things we're going to discover, the tools and methods for navigating uncertainty and finding fulfilment at work – the things that I used to inform my career change – are entirely universal. It doesn't matter if you're questioning your career for the first time, job-hopping for the fifth time or stuck in a dead-end gig and panicking that you've left it all too late, I'm confident there's something in here for you.

Whether that's helping you uncover what 'success' really means for you, or making you realise that there's always time to change course, or helping you to square your choices with friends and family, what follows should be helpful. At the very least, I'd like you to know that you're not alone.

One small caveat is that, if you're expecting the conventional self-help stuff, I'm afraid you'll be disappointed. Books about jobs tend to peddle a dream of less work, higher earnings and early retirement. And, while I love the idea of earning millions by writing a blog for 20 minutes every other Tuesday, the plan here is to dig a little deeper. I want to prod and poke the tropes, with a cynic's eye, to see what's really going on. Is it *really* never too late to change careers? Is money *really* a bad way to measure success? Is side hustling *really* a viable option?

It's also honest. I'm no guru or sage or Svengali. And while I've spent months speaking to bosses, psychologists, career specialists and normal people – men and women of different ages, ethnicities, industries and geographies – I don't pretend to have it all figured out. I'm not 'cured' of career concerns. I still struggle often with mental health. I still have days when I wake up thinking I've made horrific career choices. It's just that those days are much, much less frequent than they used to be. Plus, I've developed something of a toolkit for dealing with them, which I look forward to sharing with you later.

Above all, though, I hope to show you that a happy work life is within reach. If you're bored, or broken, or feeling pointless, or underpaid, or not being paid at all, I want you to know that your predicament is temporary.

Fulfilling, paid work is possible and it's possible for you.

You don't need to be a polo-necked billionaire in Silicon Valley to discover your professional purpose, and you certainly don't need meal replacement shakes, 4am wake-ups or an overseas personal assistant to realise it. All you need is a degree of curiosity, an openness to explore risk and a willingness to commit. Oh, and the occasional visit to a graveyard, of course.

ARE YOU A DRIFTER?

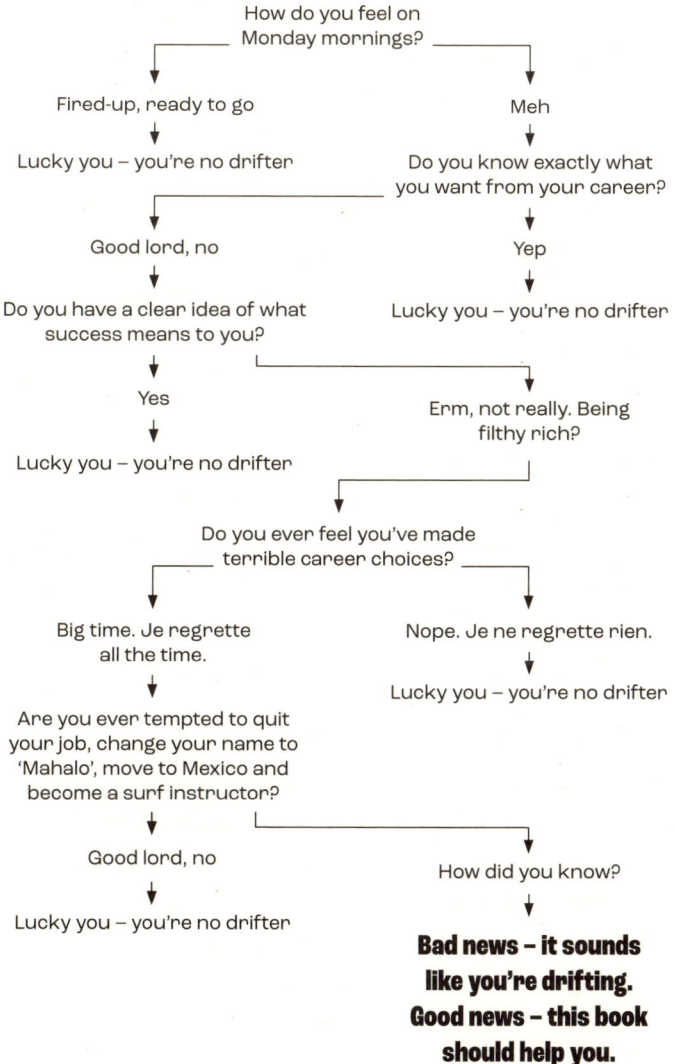

How do you feel on Monday mornings?

Fired-up, ready to go
↓
Lucky you – you're no drifter

Meh
↓
Do you know exactly what you want from your career?
↓
Yep
↓
Lucky you – you're no drifter

Good lord, no
↓
Do you have a clear idea of what success means to you?
↓
Yes
↓
Lucky you – you're no drifter

Erm, not really. Being filthy rich?

Do you ever feel you've made terrible career choices?

Big time. Je regrette all the time.
↓
Are you ever tempted to quit your job, change your name to 'Mahalo', move to Mexico and become a surf instructor?
↓
Good lord, no
↓
Lucky you – you're no drifter

Nope. Je ne regrette rien.
↓
Lucky you – you're no drifter

How did you know?
↓
Bad news – it sounds like you're drifting. Good news – this book should help you.

WHY ARE WE DRIFTING?

ONE OF THE quirks of having written a book about a breakdown is that, from time to time, companies and conferences invite you to speak about it. Perhaps it's 'Time to Talk' Day or they're announcing a new mental health policy and so, in return for some dosh and the promise of some pre-orders, I'll potter over and talk about crying in the bogs.

At the start it was quite nerve-racking, but nowadays I really enjoy it. After all, it's interesting to visit different companies, the HR people are usually lovely and, put plainly, I need the dosh. Sometimes, though, you chance upon a stinker. Perhaps the email didn't go out early enough so no one attends, or maybe you forget your lines, or perhaps someone in the audience drifts off to sleep.

One incident that comes to mind happened at a conference back in 2020. I shan't name the event, but if you've worked in the corporate world for more than a year you've doubtless attended something similar.

I must admit that I was flattered to have been asked. My book had only been out for a few months and I hadn't done many big conferences (or small ones for that matter). So when the opportunity came to sit on a panel thing, I said yes immediately. The session was called something nonsensical like 'The Future of the Future' or 'Workplace 6.0', and alongside me there was a nice lady from a university, someone from Google (you could spot him because he had clear-framed specs) and the Marketing Director of whichever company had paid to sponsor the event. He was a 40-ish-year-old man with a Paul Smith shirt and an iPad, who opened the session by saying, 'I guess I'm the only thing between you guys and a beer, right?' Never a good sign.

In the briefing email from the week before, I'd been told to prepare some thoughts about mental health at work. But, the moment the session started, it became apparent that Mr Marketing Director had other plans. 'So Josh,' he said, turning to me, 'you're a millennial. Why is it that people your age are so impatient, narcissistic and entitled in work?'

Of course, I'd love to say that, in a flash, I responded with a quick-witted, nuanced and statistically proven retort. But in reality I just froze, stared at my notes and mumbled something about the credit crunch until the nice lady from the university saved me. It was an unedifying experience and on the train home I resolved to get to the bottom of the 'millennial question'. Which sounds easy, but is actually very tricky, if only because there are loads of us. Indeed, using the classic definition (those born between 1980 and 2000) there are over 1.8 billion millennials in existence today. How can you begin drawing conclusions and generalities about a group so vast?

Then there's the problem that much of the research into younger people – particularly the stuff about work – is pretty flimsy. Sample sizes are often woefully small, survey designs lack rigour and vested interests abound. It's little wonder, for example, that research from an e-learning company finds that the best way to engage younger workers is to offer them . . . e-learning. Whereas research from a pension provider finds that what most people want from employers is . . . a pension.

So what *do* we know about young people and their plight?

Well, when it comes to folks in developed countries, there's plenty of hard data to suggest that we're poorer than our predecessors. Throughout the last few hundred years, wages in developed countries have steadily grown for each successive generation. Even through the turbulence of the thirties and the turmoil of World War Two, each cohort of new workers earned steadily more than the one before it. That is until the eighties when, courtesy of things like low productivity growth and the de-unionisation of workers, the trend stalled.

In just a few short years, what had once seemed like a natural, inevitable consequence of economic development suddenly ground to a halt. Wages stagnated. And as a result of this stagnation, people in their thirties today have, for the first time, lower household incomes than those born during the previous decade.

This disheartening trend is common across most Western democracies, but it's felt particularly acutely in the UK. Not only do Brits earn less than many of our European and American counterparts, but our costs of living are also higher. Whereas a Spanish or Austrian 20-something might spend about £90 a month travelling to work, in the UK that figure is closer to £135. Similarly, rents in London are nearly double those in other European cities like Copenhagen or Milan.

In addition to being paid less, younger workers are also less employed. Either we're unemployed and don't have jobs at all, or we're *under*employed and work part-time or in gigs that don't match our skills; architects cleaning loos, that sort of thing. And, sadly, both factors – unemployment and underemployment – have got worse since the coronarvirus showed up. For example, a recent (and decent) study by Deloitte found that nearly 25 per cent of 25–30-year-olds had either lost their jobs because of the pandemic or been placed on temporary, unpaid leave. That's much higher than the percentage of older workers who've suffered the same fate.

When the axe falls, it usually falls on younger workers.

So we're lower paid and less employed. Anything else? Yes. We're also more indebted than our parents (thanks largely to university tuition fees and debts) and much less likely to own a home. Which is to say nothing of our loneliness, anxiety and rates of depression which – surprise, surprise – also exceed those of our elders. Hooray!

The structural realities facing us are, then, pretty grim. But the question remains of what – if we're lucky enough to be in a job – we're like at work. Are we really 'unmanageable'? Are we really, as the popular belief suggests, entitled, narcissistic, self-interested, scatty and lazy?

The answer here – and I'm glad to finally be delivering some good news – is a big, fat, unqualified, unalloyed 'no'. Contrary to all those thousands of think pieces and *Newsnight* debates, we can say definitively that there is no hard evidence, statistical proof or quantitative data to support the argument that millennials are more entitled or lazy than their predecessors. None whatsoever.

In fact, I could find only one study which even attempts to make this claim statistically. But, like much of the research, it's deeply flawed because it views us in isolation, rather than comparing us to older generations when they were our age. It's one thing to say that young workers are more entitled than older ones, but it's an entirely different thing to suggest that this trend is new or specific to *today's* workers. As researcher Amanda Kreun says, 'Young people today tend to see themselves and their work environments in a similar way as did young people from previous generations.'

That's how we see ourselves, though. What about how others see us? Here the picture gets a little nuanced. In almost all my conversations with older bosses, words like 'impatient', 'demanding' and 'underdressed' have come up. But – and it's a big 'but' – this is nothing new. For time immemorial, or certainly since the Romans, older generations have poked fun or even despaired at their successors.

As George Orwell said, 'Every generation imagines itself to be more intelligent than the one that went before it, and wiser than the one that comes after it.'

To see this intergenerational disdain in action you need only compare, as journalist Sarah Kessler does, the news stories of the nineties and noughties. This reveals that the media's treatment of young workers today is an almost carbon copy of how they used to view the generation before us (aka Generation X, who were born between the sixties and eighties). For example, when *Time* magazine recently led with a cover story headlined 'Millennials: The me me me generation', they no doubt thought they were being original. In reality, however, *The Washington Post* ran a story with the exact same sentiments in reference to the Gen Xers 20 years earlier: 'The boring twenties: Grow up, crybabies, you're America's luckiest generation' read their scornful headline.

And the copying and pasting of yesterday's gripes doesn't end there. Just like us, Gen Xers were also decried as 'slackers' who 'sleep in their clothes' and 'moan about the national debt they've inherited'. They were also condemned for preferring 'more flexible schedules' and seeing 'no reason why they can't have fun in the office'. And for being 'impatient', and 'lazy', and 'confused', and 'apathetic'. Sound familiar?

But if the popular sentiments associated with young workers are neither new nor based on any quantitative data, why have they caught on? Of course, there are lots of reasons, but chiefly it's because humans crave simplicity. When faced with complexity we default to stereotype. We, as Robert Jay

Lifton says, try to reduce things into 'brief, highly reductive, definitive-sounding phrases, easily memorized and easily expressed'. In other words, we love a cliché.

We also have a mass media obsessed with controversy and stoking intergenerational tension. Pick up any newspaper today and you'll find countless column inches devoted to sneering, unevidenced, insidious claptrap pitching young people against their elders. Whether it's destroying the institution of marriage, owning too many houseplants or refusing to use napkins, there's always some reason to be angry at people under 40. And that anger seems to have leached into workplace attitudes, too.

This is not to say, however, that our working habits and 'wants' are the exact same as those of older generations. Indeed, while there's no evidence that we're more entitled, lazy or narcissistic, there *is* evidence to suggest that we want different things from our jobs. We care much more about the externalities of our work. We want our jobs and employers to care about the climate, the environment and diversity in a way that older workers don't (and previous generations didn't). We also crave flexibility, autonomy and opportunities to develop, learn and progress.

Of all of our wants, it's that last one – a desire for learning and development – which seems to be the most important. Without exception, everyone I've spoken to, from CEOs to young workers themselves, have stressed it. 'Younger employees want to know you've got a plan for them,' said Simon Longbottom, CEO of Stonegate Pubs (which employs roughly 6,000 workers under 40). 'If you don't, they'll leave.

It's as simple as that.' And he's right. Aside from pay, the two biggest reasons why young workers quit jobs are a lack of progression or a clear roadmap for growth and insufficient learning and development.

So that's what we want from our employers. The problem is that very few of us are getting it. According to Gallup, only 29 per cent of us are engaged at work and 60 per cent of us are currently looking for alternative jobs. Which isn't an empty threat, by the way. We're not just idle moaners – when we say we'll leave, as Deloitte found, we leave.

I must stress that it's not all doom and gloom. Some of the news regarding young people and work is hugely positive. We are, for example, extremely resilient. Despite the various crises/general psychodrama of the past decade, we've largely held ourselves with steel and determination. Which is to say nothing of our entrepreneurialism – when life gave us lemons, many young people launched lemonade businesses (much more on this later).

But nevertheless, it is curious that, for so many of us, 'conventional' work doesn't seem to be working. In the past 50 years of human history, we've made incredible progress in almost all areas of our well-being. Our collective ingenuity has doubled life expectancy, more than halved child mortality and quadrupled average incomes. And yet, when it comes to our jobs, almost all measures of workplace well-being have got worse. Why?

OPTION 1: MODERN WORK IS JUST BORING

An obvious starting point for exploring why modern work seems so unfulfilling is to ask whether, well, modern work is simply unfulfilling. Maybe, after centuries of inexorable technological change, the jobs left for young workers are just dull. Perhaps being unfulfilled, bored and uncertain is a fact of modern life in advanced, capitalist economies.

Certainly that's what David Graeber (the anthropologist I mentioned earlier) thought. For him, the proliferation of boring and pointless jobs – 'bullshit jobs' as he called them – is an implicit and impactful consequence of capitalism. There were two main reasons why Graeber thought this. The first is to do with class politics and a ruling elite terrified of what would happen if workers worked less. This shadowy group of capitalist overlords have decided that 'a happy and productive population with free time on their hands' is 'a mortal danger'. And so, to avoid us grubby proles getting up to no good, they've invented streams of pointless jobs to keep us occupied. After all, as every member of the illuminati knows, the devil makes work for idle millennials.

Graeber's second explanation for the explosion in 'bullshit jobs' is to do with managers. More specifically, managers who hire underlings to make themselves seem important. In a world where 'number of direct reports' is seen as a proxy for importance, the obvious strategy for managers with hiring power is to recruit as many people as possible, regardless of whether there's anything for them to do.

It's this second argument that, to my mind at least, is more convincing. And not just because I've seen this kind of forlorn empire-building throughout my career. But also because – don't judge me – I've done it myself. Awful, I know. But only once, and only at a microscopic level. Just the one hubristic hire for me. And to be fair, I didn't have much of a choice. I mean, what was I supposed to say when my boss asked if I needed 'help with my workload'? 'Oh no, absolutely not, Steve! The last thing I need is any help. I spent most of yesterday playing Candy Crush and snoozing in the bogs.'

But beyond class politics and my ego, there are also structural reasons why so many modern jobs are unfulfilling. Mostly it's to do with the unrelenting division and specialisation of labour, which has left us with jobs that are highly specific and highly dull.

Modern businesses are much, much more complicated than those of yesteryear. Supply chains are longer, financing arrangements are more intricate, working hours are more flexible, and so on. None of which is necessarily a bad thing. In fact, globalisation and complexity are usually *good* things, because they deliver lower prices and bring wealth to emerging markets. But they're also, as *The Economist* suggests, 'an enormous pain to manage'. And in order to manage this complexity, we've had to create tons and tons of really niche – sometimes 'single-task' – jobs that 'are the modern equivalent of the industrial line worker'. Yesterday's cotton loomer is, it seems, today's telesalesman.

Of course, economically, there can be huge benefits to specialisation. It enables companies to perform different tasks simultaneously, rather than consecutively. And over time it leads to workers who are specialists, rather than generalists. But the problem is that humans want to be generalists. We hate specialisation and repetition. They're the very antithesis of what it means to live a good life. We want variety, to be excited, to be challenged, to *learn*. Not to sit about doing the same things, attending the same meetings, eating the same lunch over and over.

And, more than that, we want to see the point of our work. That's what's so pernicious about much of modern employment. Lots of things in life are dull and repetitive – brushing your teeth, tax returns, dinner parties – but at least there's a reason for doing them. With lots of jobs nowadays that isn't the case. They're both repetitive *and* pointless. Or at least that's how it seems to us specialised workers unsure of how our role fits into the bigger picture.

The impacts of monotony and pointlessness on our mental health are profound. In the short term they lower mood, raise anxiety and cause despair. Which, incidentally, is why throughout history they've been such effective tortures. It's unsurprising, for example, that of all the horrors of the Yugoslavian prison camps, one of the most effective ways to break prisoners was forcing them to carry boulders from one place to another, only to tell them, when finished, to take them back.

In the longer term, too, boredom at work has been correlated with declining cognitive function in later life. According to researchers from the University of Florida, the brain is a muscle which withers without use. Their study, which analysed over 5,000 workers, found a close correlation between workplace stimulation and cognitive ability. The more monotonous someone's job, the worse their long-term brain function. Being bored today, it seems, can make us forgetful and slow tomorrow.

A further, final implication of professional specialisation is that it makes us feel trapped. Once we've developed our niche area of expertise – be it a specific branch of medicine, a curious piece of software or a particular engineering specialism – the idea of changing direction seems irresponsible, if not impossible. I've heard this in countless conversations with fellow workers. 'I spent so many years training, I can't walk away now' is a common sentiment. Along with 'I only know this specific programme' and 'I don't have any contacts in other industries'.

As I hope to convince you later, the majority of these worries are – thank goodness – misplaced. Not only does interesting, fulfilling work exist in today's economy, it's also much more attainable than you might think. But to the worker stuck down a career cul de sac, that's irrelevant. They think they're trapped – that's their perception – and the resulting anxiety and despair are very much real.

OPTION 2: WE EXPECT MORE FROM WORK

Ask any evolutionary scientist why humans rule the earth, and doubtless they'll say it's due to our brains. Not just the size of them; although, relative to our bodies, we do have much bigger brains than most other animals. But also the make-up of our brains. Or, more specifically, the fact that we have a much larger prefrontal cortex – the area of the brain responsible for 'executive functions' like decision-making and, crucially, the ability to imagine. Other animals can't do this. Yes, they can spot danger and, like Pavlov's dogs, they identify cause and effect. But they don't have ideas. They can't predict the future like we can. And it's this capability which has turned out to be humankind's evolutionary superpower. It's what has enabled us to create laws, and corporations, and property rights, and so much more besides. Our imaginations are why, according to Yuval Noah Harari in his book *Sapiens: A Brief History of Humankind*, humans 'rule the world' while 'ants eat our leftovers and chimps are locked up in zoos'.

But there's also a problem with our imagination. Namely, that it's really bad at predicting our future happiness.

Push the human brain to determine what will make us happy and by how much, and it almost always gets it wrong.

If, for example, I asked you to predict which of two life events – winning the lottery and losing a leg – would make you more happy, I'm willing to guess that you'd opt for the lottery win. Closing your eyes, you'd imagine a big house, a fast car and not having to work again, and think that'd make you happy. Or, at the very least, happier than if you'd lost a leg. 'Make me a millionaire,' you'd say. 'That'll cheer me up.' But, you'd be wrong. Indeed, as a now infamous study in Illinois found, after a year, recent paraplegics actually exhibited the same or higher levels of happiness than lottery winners.

This sounds counter-intuitive, but it actually makes sense. What happens is that, following a temporary spike in satisfaction immediately after winning, the newly minted millionaires settle into a new normal. As the researchers said, they 'become accustomed to the additional pleasures made possible by their new wealth'. And so after a few months of fancy dinners and lavish holidays, the things which used to make them sad start to do so again. Winning the lottery doesn't cure them of their insecurities, vulnerabilities and weaknesses. And that fact starts to make them sad.

In contrast, the paraplegics actually gain happiness because their experience turns out to be better than they expected. After the shock and despair of their accident, they begin to discover that many of life's great pleasures are still available to them. They can still enjoy their friends, and listen to great music, and eat fantastic food, and appreciate a good view. Life isn't so bad after all. And as they begin to realise this, their levels of satisfaction rise.

Setting high expectations for ourselves and each other is, of course, crucial in a well-functioning society. It's why we wear deodorant, and open doors, and split the bill. These are good things. The problem, however, comes when our expectations aren't met. When our over-egged estimates of future happiness collide with underwhelming realities, the resulting gap makes us sad, anxious and oftentimes angry. This is true of everything, from disappointing holidays to mediocre marriages; but nowhere is the psychological toll of missed expectations higher than in our work.

There are few things more soul-destroying in life than showing up to a new job, or getting a promotion, only to discover that it's not what you expected. With the exception of Storyteller Media, I've felt this sensation in every job I've had. In my experience, the creeping doubt – 'Is this really what I want to be doing?' – sets in after a few days. Within a month I know for sure. And from there it's just a question of how long I can last. How many eight-hour days can I grind out in that chilling, hollow void between the job I thought I was getting and the one that I got?

It's rubbish, but it's also nothing new. For years, people have been showing up to work expecting to change the world, only to discover that their role is actually terribly dull. But the problem does seem particularly acute now. For example, a recent study found that of the 33 per cent of workers who quit their jobs within the first 90 days, nearly half of them said it was because the day-to-day role wasn't what they'd expected. Which explains why, according to jobsite Indeed, a staggering 65 per cent of people look for new jobs only three months after having started their current one.

Why are people's expectations of work not being met? The answer here is twofold. Firstly, as we saw just now, much modern work just is a bit disappointing. The tedium of single-task, highly specialised jobs results in dismally dull realities which would be outstripped by even the most modest expectations.

But on the other side of the equation, it's also possible that our expectations of work have grown taller. Maybe, where our parents saw a job as a series of tasks you did for money, we see them as something much more important. And if they turn out not to be, maybe that's what makes us quit or feel anxious and worried. Sounds plausible, but the evidence here is nuanced. It's not that our expectations of work are higher, it's that they're *different*.

When our parents and grandparents demanded more from work, they tended to ask for tangible things – higher pay, better conditions, more holidays, and so on. By today's standards these may seem simple, but this is to their favour. Because by being simple, these worker demands are also quantifiable. We can measure things like wages, and holiday allowances, and notice periods; and, as a result, we can track progress against these objectives. It also allows us to know when our expectations have been met. With our modern – more intangible – expectations of work, that isn't the case. What level of 'professional purpose' is enough, for instance? What amount of 'workplace diversity' is satisfactory? How will we know when an employer is 'environmentally conscious' enough? And anyway, how are you defining 'environmentally conscious'?

Because we can't quantify modern expectations of work, we can't know if they're being met. Worse, over time, what we expect can shift unknowingly. Like the lottery winners in Illinois, the positive impact from a boost in 'professional purpose' or 'opportunities to learn' (say from a promotion or new job) quickly becomes absorbed into a new, more ambitious baseline.

This is not to say that younger workers are wrong to set high expectations for employers. In fact, quite the opposite is true. If we're to reverse the wrongs of the past – culturally, politically, economically, environmentally – then businesses must be held to higher standards. And employees (alongside shareholders, the press and governments) must play a big role in doing so. But the intangibility of our modern professional expectations is nevertheless a challenge. It's as though we're desert explorers chasing a mirage called 'fulfilment' which, no matter how hard we try to move towards it, seems to vanish further into the distance. We have no way of knowing when we've reached it and no concept of how far we've come, and both of those facts make us unhappy.

But why? Why do we expect different things from work? There are a number of factors at play here.

Firstly, the obvious one: the reason our parents and grandparents cared more about basic pay and working conditions was because they had to. Employment law – in the UK at least – didn't really exist until the sixties. As a result, our predecessors were forced to set their expectations against basic needs like wages, conditions and holidays. Nowadays, thankfully, most of these factors are taken as read. We've got the minimum wage, statutory sick pay and laws about discrimination; and this allows us to set our sights higher. It allows us to focus on less tangible things like environmentalism and diversity.

We've also got far more choice when it comes to jobs. And because of this, we've grown pickier and got used to expecting more. Back in the day, your career choice was largely determined by geography. If you were born in Glasgow, you built ships. If you were born in Birmingham, you built cars. If you were born in Woking – as I was – you stole cars. And so on. Nowadays, none of those rules apply. Now it's entirely possible to live in Manchester but commute to Birmingham, or live in New York but work Berlin hours, from home.

Plus the nature of many jobs has changed. Nowadays most people can do most jobs. That sounds like a bold statement, but it's true. Yes, every job entails some specific knowledge or lingo. But the commonalities between roles (particularly those done by younger workers) far outweigh the differences. With a few weeks' training, an IT Manager could easily become a Procurement Lead, or a Digital Marketing Assistant, or a Public Relations Officer. After all, at their core, what do these jobs really entail? Sending emails, attending meetings and solving problems. Which are real skills, but they're also highly transferable. And this, combined with our ever-shrinking world, has massively broadened our professional field of vision. It's furnished us with more options and avenues than ever before. And, consequently, we've become choosier – our expectations of what a job should give us have grown taller – while, at the same time, the realities of much work have grown grimmer.

Then there's our parents.

OPTION 3: OUR PARENTS SCREWED US UP

Isn't it depressing how the adverts you get served online change as you grow older? I noticed it through my twenties, but it was most noticeable when I turned 30. Where once I used to get perky pop-ups trying to flog me trendy trainers or 'hot singles in my area', now they're only ever about two things: business advice and boner pills. Either I'm being persuaded to invest in cryptocurrency or I'm being sold a dream of endless, monster erections. Of the two, I think I'd rather have the Bitcoin.

The reason I bring this up is because it was through one of these business-y digital adverts that I first came across Simon Sinek. He's one of those TED Talkin', bestsellin', future gazin', 'opinion-havers for hire' whose videos, to use the modern parlance, tend to 'go viral'. The one that I got advertised was called 'Simon Sinek on millennials in the workplace' and if you've spent more than a minute on YouTube you've doubtless seen it yourself. Indeed, at the time of writing, the video has 12 million views, over 110,000 likes and nearly 7,000 shares. And it's easy to see why.

In the video, Simon monologues, with eloquence and confidence, about the plight of young workers. 'You have an entire generation which is growing up with lower self-esteem than previous generations,' he says, before listing off all the reasons why. Chief of which – he reckons – is our parents. Or rather the 'failed parenting strategies' our parents used in raising us.

The problem, Sinek argues, is that, throughout our upbringings, us younger workers were told that we 'were special all the time' and that 'we can have anything in life, just because [we] want it'. Worse, some of us got A grades because our teachers 'didn't want to deal with the parents'. And we even got awarded 'participation medals – medals for coming in last'. All of which was bad. Very, very bad indeed. Because in encouraging us to set high expectations for our lives, what our parents actually did was, apparently, set us up for a miserable fall. 'The moment they were thrust into the real world,' Simon says, 'they discovered that they weren't special, that their moms couldn't get [them] a promotion, that you get nothing for coming in last and, by the way, you can't just have it because you want it.' And it's this brutal, crushing realisation that has left so many of us unhappy, unfulfilled, anxious and depressed.

Lovely stuff. And, importantly, stuff that sort of seems to make sense. There's little question that, having received austere, near-Victorian upbringings themselves, our parents wanted to give us the opposite. They wanted us to feel safe and comfortable and loved. But maybe it went too far. Maybe in their attempts to protect and care for us, what our parents actually did was create a generation of cossetted, overly precious snowflakes incapable of dealing with the harsh realities of life.

So convincing is this theory that in recent years it's become something of an accepted wisdom. You hear it not only on YouTube videos and at business conferences, but also at dining tables and in coffee shops. And yet, counter arguments do exist.

Take, for example, the fact that, for this theory to work, we'd all have to have been raised in the same way. Or at least, most of us would have to have been raised in a substantially similar way. This just isn't the case. There are roughly two billion sets of parents in the world and each of them raises their children differently. Kids in Sydney have very different upbringings to kids in rural Scotland, who in turn are raised differently to those in Chicago. Which is to say nothing of the variations within specific postcodes, or streets, or even apartment buildings. If a universal, homogenised 'parenting strategy' doesn't exist, how can it possibly explain our shared workplace woes?

The second issue is that the evidence against that style of parenting is more complex than the theory suggests. Yes, on the one hand, a bunch of psychologists suggest that positive reinforcement (telling your kids they're great) is bad. But, on the other hand, there are also plenty who say it's good. Put plainly, the only scientific, psychological and sociological consensus is a blindingly obvious one. That is: different children react differently to different parenting styles.

However, this is not to say that our parents had no impact on our attitudes towards life and work. It's just that their influence is more nuanced and complicated than the dominant theory suggests. In part, yes, our parents' parenting styles taught us to actively set high expectations of life and work. But they also taught us to do so more passively, through a kind of osmosis. Growing up in the eighties, nineties and noughties, we saw our elders' incomes rising, their rate of homeownership increasing and their stock portfolios booming and – without thinking about it – assumed that things would be the same for us. When 'the Boomers' were at the peak of their careers from 1981 to 2001, average incomes rose by 78 per cent. And witnessing this imbued us with a natural confidence about our futures. One which, as we discovered on entering the workforce, turned out to be entirely misplaced. Because, as it happens, wage growth isn't a given, home ownership isn't guaranteed and GDP growth isn't inevitable.

And it's *this* realisation – that we arrived at the party at the exact moment the police shut it down – plus all the stuff about us being mollycoddled and fragile, which has contributed to our collective disappointment with work.

Our parents and their example taught us to expect more, but reality had a different plan.

OPTION 4: SOCIAL MEDIA MADE US HATE WORK

On average I scroll social media for four hours a day. Dusting off my GCSE maths calculator I can tell you that's equivalent to 28 hours a week or 60 days a year. In fact, it's about a sixth of every year that I spend mindlessly thumbing my way around the Internet. Bonkers, really. Particularly given that *I know that social media makes me unhappy.* Worse, I've written a book and several articles about how bad it is. I've done talks, and podcasts, and conferences urging people to give it up. And yet, the moment I collapse onto the sofa or sit on the bus, out comes my iPhone and up pops Instagram.

Often I justify the scrolling by telling myself it's for work. 'I should really keep abreast with what's going on,' I'll say – the modern equivalent of 'one cigarette can't hurt' or 'it's only a bit of smack'. And sure enough, within 10 seconds of gawping at my newsfeed I'm entranced. My eyes glaze over, my pulse lowers, my breathing slows, time melts away.

I'm going to give social media a bit of a hammering now, but there are *some* positives. People forget that. It was, for example, really helpful and supportive when I was going through my breakdown. You have to search quite hard, but if you do, you'll find nooks of community and crannies of friendship on sites like Facebook and Instagram. We saw a similar thing during the coronavirus pandemic. Locked down, alone, isolated from each other, many of us returned to using social media as originally intended – to connect and communicate. We didn't have holidays, restaurants or parties to brag about, so instead we messaged our auntie in Canada or shared the secret to our banana bread. Mostly we just said, 'I'm still here, still trying to smile, still trying to conquer sourdough.' It was quite lovely, really – a silver lining to an otherwise horrifically dark cloud.

But, that brief interlude aside, I'm afraid that the effects of social media are grim. I expect you already knew that, but they really are. Social media is bad for our sleep, and our anxiety, and our self-esteem. And – most importantly for our careers – it's also made us much more jealous and envious of each other. This isn't surprising.

Before social media, if you wanted to get riled up about your neighbour's new car or your mate's new golf clubs, you'd have to go and see them. As in, you'd physically have to walk past their house or go to the golf club. Nowadays, you don't. Now, courtesy of the little black mirror in your pocket, you're able to experience jealousy in every moment of every day. Feeling lonely? Whack! Here's a picture of a party you weren't invited to. Feeling unmotivated? Thump! Here's a video of someone with better abs than you doing sit-ups. Hate your job? Kapow! Here's a cryptocurrency millionaire driving his Lamborghini. And on, and on. Social media has also localised envy. Whereas in the past, the objects of our aspiration were the lives of movie stars, celebrities and royals, now it's our friends who we're jealous of – their recent holiday pictures, their perfect-seeming kids, their followership. And because we know these people – because they're people like us, because they could be us – the envy is somehow intensified.

Most importantly for us, though, social media has given us a keyhole into each other's professional lives and, guess what, everyone else's professional life is better than yours. They're all getting promotions and winning awards. What are you doing? You're scrolling through LinkedIn while doing a poo, you pathetic, lazy, under-paid underachiever.

Indeed, if our elders' example taught us to set high expectations for work, it was social media which told us that everyone (apart from us) was achieving those expectations. Which they aren't. Honestly, they aren't.

Just as someone lies or misrepresents their social life on Instagram, they also distort and over-egg their professional lives on LinkedIn.

They're not really 'delighted to have spoken at SnoreCon 2.0'; or 'thrilled to be named a rising star at the Tosser Awards 2020'; or 'excited to be discussing all things "haulage" on Derek McDull's podcast'. Instead, like everyone else, they're bored, insecure and adrift. I know this because I've spoken to lots of these people. Folks whose careers look fantastic on LinkedIn, but who, the moment you ask 'how's work?', reveal their ennuied reality.

A conversation with my friend Annie illustrated this perfectly. I've known Annie for years and she spent the first 10 years of her career in financial services. She's confident, personable and fun; and, refracted through social media, her six-figure career in the City looks about as perfect as you might imagine. She's always on trips to New York, and having meetings in Berlin, and taking clients to the rugby. And, without fail, every 18 months, LinkedIn invites me to 'Congratulate Annie on her promotion'.

'What's your new book about?' she asked during a coronavirus-mandated walk.

'Oh, it's not one for you,' I said. 'It's about people our age who are unhappy in work.'

'What do you mean?' she exclaimed. 'You do know I've just quit?'

In the conversation that followed I discovered that she'd hated her job for at least three years. It had been fun in the beginning, but as the work got harder and the hours got longer, the doubt started to creep in. Then slowly the unhappiness at work started leaching into her personal life. She stopped exercising, her booze intake crept up and she began putting on weight. She also, for the first time, started having trouble sleeping. Which seemed to be the final straw.

'Eventually they gave me three weeks off for "stress",' she said. 'I was completely burned out.'

'But . . . but,' I spluttered, 'what about all that stuff on LinkedIn? What about that award? Didn't you just get promoted?'

'Ha ha,' came the reply. 'Don't believe everything you see on social media.'

The problem is that we do. We believe it all and it's making us really unhappy. In fact, according to Ethan Kross, Professor of Psychology at the University of Michigan, social media is exerting a 'toll on us, the likes of which we have never experienced in the history of our species'. We'll explore what we can do about social media, envy and 'comparisoni-tis' in much greater detail later. But for now, just know that it's one of the biggest contributors to our lack of workplace fulfilment. It's a central tenet in that looming, spectral sense that we've ballsed-up our careers. 'Everyone else's grass is greener,' it tells us, 'and it's all your fault.'

WHY DO WE DRIFT?

Back in the day

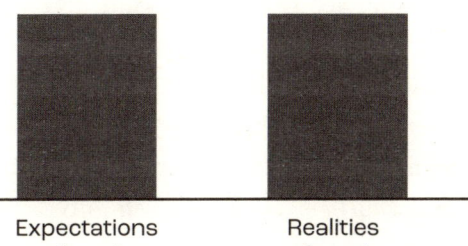

Expectations
of work

Realities
of work

Nowadays

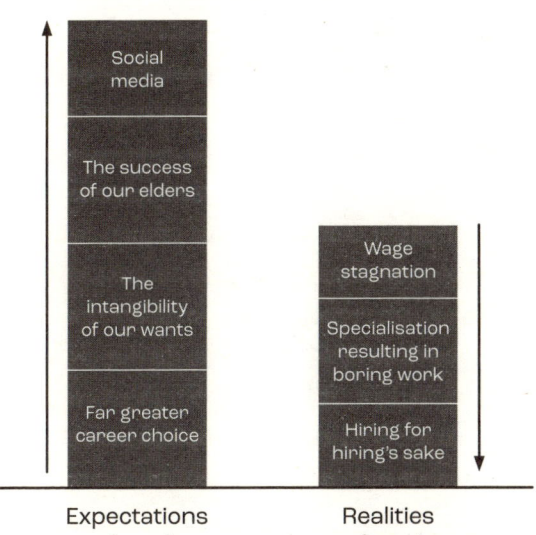

Social
media

The success
of our elders

The
intangibility
of our wants

Far greater
career choice

Wage
stagnation

Specialisation
resulting in
boring work

Hiring for
hiring's sake

Expectations
of work

Realities
of work

Putting all this together it's easy to see why the causes of our generational drift are more complex and nuanced than the clichés suggest. It's not that we're impatient, entitled narcissists; we just expect different things from work. Things that are less tangible, harder to measure and harder to know you've achieved. That isn't our fault. It's also not our fault that we grew up seeing the generation in front of us doing well and expected the same for ourselves. Or that social media just happened to explode at the exact moment when we were entering the workplace, amplifying our expectations yet further. Or that – and this is the big one – all our new, elevated expectations came to fruition at the exact moment when the economy collapsed and work grew more specialised and dull.

That's what's happened. That's *why* we drift. Now let's see what we can do about it.

HAVE I LEFT IT TOO LATE?

THERE COMES A sobering moment in everyone's life when they realise that, were they to enter TV's *The X Factor*, they'd be lumped into the 'over 25s' category. If you've never watched the show, you mightn't realise what that means. 'What's so bad about being 26?' you might think. 'Isn't that still quite young?' But you'd be wrong. So wrong. In fact, you couldn't be wrong-er. For in the world of reality TV, nothing is more unsightly than someone over the age of 25 trying to make a change. It doesn't matter if you've got a great voice, perky dance moves or – deep breath here – lots of 'star quality', once you're past 25, you're past *it*. The problem is that, when it comes to our careers, most of society seems to agree.

In part, we do it to ourselves. Even amongst my peers there's this curious mantra that, as we enter our late twenties, our professional die is cast. Once the clock strikes 12 on our 26th birthdays, we're frozen in time, petrified in our final professional form. We're trapped, unable to switch or change our careers, confined to whichever narrow path we fell onto on leaving school or university. I've lost count of the number of people who've voiced some version of this to me: 'I've worked in sales for 10 years, so that's all I know', or 'I'm not really enjoying medicine, but I've done all the training now', or 'I wish I'd gone for a higher earning career, but never mind, it's too late'.

But we also do it to each other. As a society, our attitudes towards career changes are desperately antiquated. At best, we view career shifts or pivots with bemused curiosity ('She's only just qualified as a lawyer, and now she's becoming a teacher?!'). At worst, we regard them as professional promiscuity, weakness or a signal of indecisiveness. Perhaps it's born of jealousy or maybe it harks back to a time when life expectancy was lower, meaning you only had time for one career. Either way, the important thing is that we stop thinking like this. Because the simple fact is that we're going to spend 50 years (or more) of our lives working, and over that time what we want from work is going to change. Human desires, interests and passions are dynamic, not static. And confronted with this inevitable evolution, we're faced with a choice: either we can deny it, pretend it isn't happening and stay stuck in jobs which no longer meet our wants (if they ever did in the first place) or we can accept it, welcome it and do something about it. Of the two, I strongly suggest we plump for the latter.

'But it's too late!'

No, it isn't. It really isn't. It can't be. I've spoken to too many people who've made successful 'later years' career switches to believe otherwise. And, in a way, I've even done it myself. At 26 I was working in advertising, four years later I'm writing this book. I earn less money, have fewer colleagues and less of an obvious career path. Plus, at the time I handed in my notice, I was terrified about stepping into the abyss. But – without wishing to seem smug – I'm delighted with the outcome. If you're considering changing lanes, chances are you'll feel the same.

Obviously, there are some notable exceptions to the 'never too late' rule. If you're in your thirties or forties, you probably won't play for Manchester United or be a piano prodigy. And I'm also not suggesting that changing careers is frictionless. Like anything in life, there are barriers and challenges which have to be overcome (and we'll explore these in detail shortly). But overcoming the practical challenges is the easy bit. Or at least, it's the 'easier than you think' bit. The really tricky part is mindset. Changing jobs requires us to change our attitudes to work, success and fulfilment. And that's tough.

Consider, for example, the story of Robert Carting. Now in his fifties, Robert started his career in the civil service before moving into accounting. 'It was just what you did,' Robert told me. 'Join the biggest company you could and get your head down.' Which is exactly the path he followed. And, as it happens, he was very good at getting his head down. In fact, he was so good that after only seven years Robert was made a Partner – pretty much the pinnacle of a career in accounting. The usual trappings of success soon followed. There was the fancy car, the big house in Surrey, the sailing holidays, the school fees. The only problem was that Robert despised it.

Partly he hated the culture which he describes as 'medieval, feudal and hugely partisan'. But mostly he'd just grown tired of it. After 22 years of long weeks, late nights and 'living on adrenaline', wouldn't you? So Robert quit. 'I was absolutely terrified,' he told me. 'I knew it was the right thing to get out, but I didn't know what to do.'

The months that followed were tricky – the emails dried up, the phone didn't ring, the diary seemed hauntingly empty. And gone, too, were the accoutrements of corporate success – British Airways downgraded his Gold card, his Hilton Honors Points expired. All of which Robert struggled with. Not because he was desperate to go and stay in a Hilton, but because it meant he was no longer 'that guy'. 'It took me a year to get over the fact that I wasn't "the Partner" anymore,' he said. 'It was so much of who I was; it was central to my self-esteem.'

After 12 months of moping around, Robert decided what he wanted to do. He'd always wanted to work in the non-profit sector, and so he started applying for roles at charities and social enterprises; roles which would pay him much, much less than his old career, but which might also not make him miserable. Eventually he got one and he hasn't looked back. 'The psychological stuff was the hardest,' he said. 'Once I'd gotten over my past and realised that it wasn't too late, I could start moving forward.'

Of course, a key difference between Robert and many young workers is that he could afford to quit. Having been a

Partner at a big corporation, he was never in danger of ending up on the streets or being unable to pay his bills. But it's a mistake to equate financial security with professional freedom. Just because someone's a Grand Fromage doesn't mean they're footloose. In fact, according to the theory of loss aversion (the idea that humans hate losing more than we enjoy gaining), you could argue that the more you earn, or the higher your career status, the *harder* it is to change jobs. There's more to lose, more at stake.

Either way, I think Robert's story teaches us two things. Mostly obviously, it shows us that it's never too late. If he could switch it up in his fifties, then you can do so in your thirties or twenties. And secondly, it shows us that often the key challenges to changing careers exist in our minds, rather than in reality. We tell ourselves it's too late, or that we don't have the skills, or that we can't turn away from our current trajectory, and so we stay put. But these aren't realities, they're excuses. Often they're welcome excuses, too. After all, most humans are inherently lazy. Given the option to strive for something difficult or settle into something easy, lots of us will opt for the latter. And, when it comes to our careers, nothing is easier than throwing our hands up, saying 'it's too late' and wallowing.

Confronting these excuses – and the fact that we all make them at some point – is crucial to overcoming inertia and uncovering fulfilling work. We have to acknowledge that, unless your dream is something that only a young person can do, everything is within our grasp. Reaching it might require re-evaluating our attitudes to work, retraining, accepting a pay cut or getting comfortable with dropping down the ladder a bit. But that's small potatoes. What we cannot do is mope around telling ourselves that our ship has sailed. Every day spent doing that is a day spent excusing our inaction.

> We must recognise that change is possible – no, probable – and commit to achieving it.

As the pioneering aviator Amelia Earhart said, 'The most difficult thing is the decision to act, the rest is merely tenacity.'

And, by the way, finding your professional rhythm when you're a bit older is actually better. As a society we fetishise youthful achievement. We love a 'Youngest person to . . .' news story – the more extreme the better. But your career is one area where you don't want to be an outlier or an extreme, because youthful success often precedes adult unhappiness. Consider, for example, the long list of former child stars who have gone on to suffer from ill mental health and substance abuse problems in later life: Demi Lovato, Shia LaBeouf, Britney Spears, and so on. Or the fact that up to 60 per cent of English Premier League players declare bankruptcy within five years of retirement (aged, on average, 35). Or, the fate of astronaut Buzz Aldrin, who battled depression and alcoholism after returning from space.

You don't want that. You don't want to be an extreme or wunderkind. Be glad that you haven't hit your peak yet. Thank goodness you weren't some child genius. Thank the

Lord you've taken some time, lived a bit and realised what you do and don't like in a job. Now you can discover fulfilment in the right, sustainable way. If that happens to be when you're 23, then great. But if you're 28, or 31, or 39, or 50 for that matter, then that's just as good.

It's also easier to find your 'forever' job when you're a bit older. You know what fires you up about work and what gets you down. You can spot whether a corporate culture is a good or bad fit. You can tell a cracking boss from a crap one.

Even if you despise your current role or have ambitions to move into a completely different industry, your career to date hasn't been wasted.

This is even more true if you're planning to start your own business. Being a little older, having been exposed to the world, makes you much more deft at spotting opportunities. You can identify problems that need solving or industries that need disrupting in a way that you couldn't if you were younger. There are countless examples of this, but one I like is Raegan Moya-Jones, who founded the luxury baby products business, aden + anais. If you haven't heard of them, they make fancy bits for babies – blankets, changing mats, towels and so forth. Their big 'thing', though, is a range of ultra-cute swaddles made from cotton muslin cloth. And it's this signature product – plus an army of celebrity endorsers – which has propelled aiden + anais to annual revenues of over £100 million and amassed Moya-Jones a sizeable fortune in the process.

It's a wonderful story, but what's really interesting is the fact that, when she launched the business, Moya-Jones had very little of what most would consider relevant experience. She hadn't worked in retail before, or designed baby clothes, or worked with suppliers. She didn't have the backing of big investors, or a shiny MBA, or an established record of building brands. What she did have, though, were 10 years working in media sales and the life experience to spot a gap in the market. Cotton muslin cloths were a staple purchase for mothers in Australia and yet, when Moya-Jones moved to the US, she couldn't find a single stockist. So, along with a friend, she resolved to make them herself. It was a simple idea but, importantly for us, it was also one that she couldn't have had in her early twenties. She had to live a little, experience the world and become a mother. Her success was born of her life experience, and if you're planning to change careers, I'm willing to bet yours will be, too.

HOW CAN I OVERCOME CAREER FEAR?

IT SEEMS AN awful truism, but making a significant change in your professional direction is going to involve compromises. Some of these will be small. Your new profession might require a longer commute, say. Or working weekends. Or wearing a suit, or not wearing a suit, or, if you're considering life as an 'influencer', wearing almost nothing at all. But there will also be bigger barriers, bigger blockers to us finding fulfilment or setting off in search of it. These are the things that make us slump into mediocrity and settle into unhappiness. In total, there are four of them, each of which is rooted in fear. They are:

1. Fear of failing (and not being able to go back)
2. Fear of losing ourselves
3. Fear of earning less
4. Fear of letting down others

These are the four horsemen of what you might call the 'careerocalypse' (sorry), and we're going to explore and unpick each in detail now. But, first, a word on fear itself . . .

Having lived much of my adult life with an anxiety disorder, I've come to know fear well. For a time, being scared and worried was a constant occupation. It was all I did. From the moment I woke up, to the second I closed my eyes, fear hung over me like some terrible, ghoulish shadow. I could worry about almost anything – from getting dumped to forgetting to breathe. Worries which might sound absurd to you were, for me, total obsessions which gave rise to an absolute, eviscerating fear. A fear which drove me to the precipice of suicide, which made me wonder if that wouldn't be easier, for me and for everyone else. A fear which forced me to consider whether not being here – *not having to be scared anymore* – would be better than living with constant, churning consternation. A fear which made me hate myself and think of myself as weak, and fragile, and useless. Why, despite the privileged fundamentals of my life, did I worry when others with far tougher lives didn't? Why was I so pathetic? Why was I so fucking useless? Why didn't I just end it, now?

And then it got better.

Not on its own. It took work. I had to stop doing some things and start doing others. I had to talk to people about it, and see a therapist, and take pills, and stop crying, and keep moving forward. And I still have to do those things today. Getting better has been the hardest, most effortful thing I've ever done (and I'm nowhere near 'done'), but it's also been the most rewarding and essential. And, perhaps most importantly, it's taught me that fear isn't singular. There isn't one 'fear' or one experience of fear. A fear of spiders is different – in structure, symptoms and treatment – to a fear of flying, which in turn varies from a fear of failure. Some fears are hot, fevered and terrifying. Others are chilling and paralysing. Some can be unpicked, dissected and treated with logic and evidence. Others require distraction. Others still demand that you accept them, live with them and grow to enjoy them.

One thing is for certain, though, fear isn't to be feared; it is to be understood. And while a litany of books and motivational speakers will tell you to 'overcome' or 'confront' or 'defeat' your fears, my (admittedly less macho) suggestion is to get to know them, get to understand their rhythms, how they feel, and what they make you do and not do.

In learning about how we experience fear – as I've discovered over the past six years – we strip it of its potency.

Jabbing and prodding your feelings and thoughts allows you to understand when and why you experience them. And from this, you can begin to develop a toolkit for moving through them, rather than being paralysed by them.

My own toolkit (which we'll explore in more detail later) contains a number of very practical things – exercising, stopping boozing, writing my thoughts down, and so on – as well as some more conceptual stuff; cognitive behavioural therapy (CBT), for example, has been something of a life-saver for me. But either way, I find that having a plan and some levers to pull gives me a great deal of comfort. It helps me stop seeing fear as a wild, uncontrolled emotion and instead regard it as a natural, evolutionary response. Above all, it enables me to put distance between myself and my fears. It helps me to acknowledge that being afraid of things doesn't make me weak, or pathetic, or fragile, it just makes me human.

FEAR OF FAILING

On the morning of 17 November 2010, Sergeant Vince Hockley was on operations in the Nahr-e Saraj area of Afghanistan. He, along with colleagues from the Irish Guards, was out meeting locals, introducing himself and building rapport. Despite a recent uptick in hostilities, the patrol seemed to be going to plan. Then, in a moment, everything changed.

'The ambush started with a single rifle shot,' Vince told me. 'Then there was a minute or so of silence before the chaos started.' And it *was* chaos. Bullets filled the air. The soldiers scrambled to find cover while returning fire. Vince watched on as shots thudded into one, then two, then three of his comrades. He was next. The .303 round tore through his buttock, femur, stomach and lung before lodging itself just below his third rib. A searing, stinging pain enveloped his body as he collapsed onto his front. From there, due to his injuries and the weight of his kit, he was unable to move. Enemy bullets continued fizzing and snapping into the ground around him, but Vince was helpless. Lying face down in the dirt, all he could do was wait – either for the rescue helicopter that would save him or the second bullet that would kill him.

It took 12 minutes for the helicopter to arrive.

Vince and his fellow soldiers were hauled aboard and transported to a nearby field hospital. And it was here that Vince died. Only momentarily, thankfully. But his heart did stop and the doctors had to rush to resuscitate him. Two emergency surgeries followed. Then a flight back to the UK during which Vince's heart failed – and was restarted – for a second time.

The next thing he remembers is waking up in Birmingham's Queen Elizabeth Hospital surrounded by his family. Unbeknown to him, the medical staff had summoned them to say their final goodbyes. But, for the fourth time in the past 48 hours, Vince had defied their predictions and lived. In the years that followed, this would become something of a running theme. People with serious faces and walls covered in diplomas would tell Vince that he couldn't achieve something; and then, within a few months, he would. Not in a swaggering, macho way – he's not one for showing off or grandstanding. It's just that, if someone says he can't do something, he wants to see if he can. 'It'll be seven months before you leave the hospital,' they said. Vince was home in three weeks. 'You'll never work for the army again,' they said. He went on to serve a further 12 years. 'You'll never walk again,' they said. He's now a fully qualified personal trainer.

There's a lot that us grey-faced, lily-livered civilians can learn from Vince. His story is one of courage, yes, as well as resilience, and perseverance, and dogged determination in the face of adversity. But the thing that really struck me from our conversation was Vince's approach to failure. Or, rather, his approach to fearing failure.

Throughout our conversation, whether he was talking about the ambush itself or his recovery, he kept repeating the idea that, when faced with a worrying or uncertain situation, he obsesses over the things that he can control and tries to ignore the things that he can't. 'If I do everything I can to the best of my ability, then that's my work done,' he says. 'The rest of it is just luck and there's no point worrying about luck.'

This is a disarmingly simple approach to fearing fear, but I like it. Unlike most self-help mantras, it doesn't try to disguise the fact that failing sucks. Because it does. Attempting something and failing – be it going into battle, applying for a job or launching a business – feels crap. It's not the revelatory, life-changing opportunity that very successful people often insist on telling us it is. It's embarrassing, and annoying, and potentially ruinous. But if you've studied your goal from every angle, worked out what you can and can't control, and done all the work, then not only is the likelihood of failure reduced, so is the fear of it.

Failure sucks much less – and is much less worthy of your fear – if you've tried your best.

Chipping away at failure, with diligence and hard work, until all that's left are the 'uncontrollables' means that whether or not we succeed is just that: uncontrollable. And uncontrollable should equal 'not-worth-worrying-about-able'. So what if your interviewer slept badly and is grouchy, or the economy implodes, or the other candidate has more years of experience, or that the law conversion course is full? All of that is beyond your influence. It's annoying, sure, but it doesn't mean anything about you as a person. Random chance happening doesn't mean you're weak, or stupid, or foolish. It doesn't mean that you're less qualified or less intelligent than others for whom random chance went the other way. Do you hate yourself when it rains? Or when you fail to win the lottery? No, of course you don't. So why would you if the job is already taken or your employer goes bust?

If you want to, you can get really practical about this. Faced with an uncertain career choice, you could write down a gigantic list of all the things that could kill your plan, ticking and crossing off those you can control and those you can't. But if you're not a pen-and-paper person, the important thing is to acknowledge that – as long as you try your best – failure is just something that happens. It's the career equivalent of a delayed train, or a traffic jam, or Thursdays. Reframing fear this way, reducing it to a series of 'can controls' and 'can't controls', somehow makes it, well, much less fearsome.

And if it does happen to you, if your business idea, or career move, or efforts to upskill fall flat on their face, then it's worth remembering the other thing that Vince taught me. Lying face down in that terrifying dirt, Vince said that two thoughts kept recurring in his mind. The first, a memory of his grandfather – something from his childhood which inexplicably kept flashing up. The second, more cerebral but no less surprising, was a relief at realising that his current situation would be the worst he'd ever experience. 'Everything from that point would be progression,' he says. 'Once I was in that helicopter and no one was shooting at me, I progressed to a better place. Once I woke up after the surgery, I progressed to a better place. And on it went.'

The lesson for us is clear: failure isn't an end, it's a beginning. If your job application gets rejected or your start-up flops, that's the start of a new phase. One in which you'll apply for new jobs or launch new businesses, all of which will mark progress. To reiterate, I'm not saying that failing is somehow great. It isn't. I've failed tons – and continue to do so – and mostly it's hard and painful. But it's also the hardest and most painful it'll ever be. From there, you can regroup, rebuild and start moving forward again.

FEAR OF LOSING OURSELVES

One of the few courses I still remember from my four years at university is a Sociology module called 'Self 101'. There are a few reasons why I remember it, but chiefly it's because the course content was unlike anything else I was studying. It was cool, and fun, and relevant for my life. As an Economics and Politics major, most of my lectures were dry, mind-numbing affairs involving demand graphs and Thomas Hobbes. But here in Sociology, all bets were off. We had tutorials about sex, and gender, and queerness, and all sorts besides. We didn't write essays, we had arguments

But we also learned stuff. Specifically, we learned how our identities as humans are constructed. We saw how every-thing – from our parents and upbringing, to our physical appearance, sexualities and class – influences how we see ourselves. And crucially, we studied how our self-image changes and gains nuance as we get older. The thing that I always remember, though, is just how important our jobs are in determining our notions of self.

What we do for money has always influenced how we define ourselves (why else would so many of our ancestors have named themselves after their professions?). But in recent decades, work has arguably become *the* determining factor in self-identity. Indeed, for many of us, what we do from 9 to 5 is the only lens through which we view ourselves.

The reason for this, according to thinkers like Anthony Giddens, is simple: in a world where the historic markers of identity (e.g. our birthplace, gender and class) have grown more fluid, work is one of the things that has remained constant. And as a result, many of us now cling to our jobs as a way of anchoring our identities.

You can see this in action all over the place, from TV game shows ('Hello Cilla, my name's Mathew and I'm a plumber from Lancashire!'), through to immigration forms and insurance quotes. Why is it, for example, that the first question we ask when we meet someone new is 'What do you do?' Is it because we're fascinated by their day-to-day lives? Do we really care about their answers? No. The only reason we do it is to acquire a convenient shorthand for their identities. 'I'm a doctor' tells us they're driven, compassionate and smart. 'I teach Year 6 Maths' tells us they're patient, caring and good at sums. 'I'm an estate agent' tells us they're, well, never mind what that tells us.

The melding between our jobs and our identities is a form of what psychologists call 'enmeshment'. Traditionally, this term describes a blurring between the personal boundaries of two people. When parents, for example, become so obsessed with their kids' success that they lose sight of their own identity, they're 'enmeshed'. But it's just as applicable to our working lives, too. To be enmeshed with our jobs means that we've ceased to exist outside of them. Our work is no longer part of our identity, it *is* our identity. Which has profound implications. It means, for example, that in hating our jobs we often end up hating ourselves. And it can also result in us staying in jobs we loathe because, in leaving that job, we lose our identities. Or that's the worry. As one person so eloquently told me, 'I hate being a nurse. But if I'm not a nurse, what am I?'

Combined, these arguments place drifters like me in an impossible conundrum. On the one hand, we hate our jobs (and consequently ourselves). But at the same time, we're fearful of leaving and compromising our identities. This is made worse by the fact that changing careers or launching businesses often entails a reduction in status. Getting in the door of a new industry or profession usually means accepting (initially at least) a lower status role. And many of us just aren't willing to accept this. 'Manager to Senior Manager, OK', our thinking goes. 'Senior Manager to Trainee? Absolutely not.'

So what to do?

Well, partly it's a case of 'put up or shut up'. It's totally fine if you're not willing to change your identity or downgrade in status, but if that is the case then you'll have to stop moaning. Harping on about how you hate your job while simultaneously doing nothing about it isn't just unhelpful for you, it's also extremely dull for everyone else.

The good news, however, is that changing identities and downgrading statuses isn't nearly as bad as you might think. Plus the longer term benefits of switching can be huge. I doubt, for example, that Jeff Bezos regrets his decision to launch Amazon, even though doing so meant going from a Senior Vice President at an investment firm to delivering orders out of the back of his car. And there are a million other stories like Jeff's. Tales of people dropping out of big-name universities or leaving fancy jobs, only to surprise their friends and families by becoming multimillionaires.

But even if you don't end up with (or lust after) a huge salary, pursuing happiness at work is still worth it. As we saw earlier, few things are more painful and depressing than spending eight hours a day bored or purposeless.

I don't care how high-status your job or how intrinsic work
is to your self-identity, spending your life miserable is too
high a price to pay.

Certainly that's been my experience.

Of the many jobs I've had, I was most 'enmeshed' with the
one at the bank. It was also the most high-status gig I've had.
Even if most days were spent snoozing or watching YouTube,
my title ('Senior Business Analyst') was quite glitzy and with
it came lots of high-status-y stuff. There was the money, obviously. But I also had an expense account, and my own desk,
and recruiters would flirt with me on LinkedIn. I despised
the job – it was a major contributor to my breakdown – but
I was also pathetically flattered by the status it afforded. It
became part of who I was. I bought clothes to go with it. I got
a new haircut. I began bringing up the topic of jobs at dinner
parties so I could boast about it. All of which made the business of walking away from it much, much harder. So what if
I was suicidal? At least I had a 400-gsm business card and
access to the underground car park.

In the end, though, the misery outweighed the trappings
of status and I quit. I dearly wish that I'd done it sooner.
Maybe, if I'd been able to look past it all, I could have escaped
before falling apart. Either way, I won't make that mistake
again. Never again will I allow professional enmeshment or
delusions of status or grandeur to obstruct the pursuit of
truly fulfilling work. Switching jobs might mean leaving a
part of you behind, but it was an unfulfilled part. Why else
would you be thinking of leaving?

FEAR OF EARNING LESS

We haven't talked much about money yet. This might seem a bit odd, given that money is an integral motivation for why we work. Even folks who really, really like their jobs wouldn't do them for free. Everyone has to pay the Wi-Fi bill and buy limescale remover.

I've left money until now for the simple reason that it's less influential than the other fears. A bold statement, perhaps, but it's true. Because money – or working out how you can get enough of it – is largely a practical thing. And practical things, as we saw earlier, are always easier to overcome than mental ones. Yes, they demand planning, diligence and a degree of humility. But this is small fry compared to, say, a paralysing fear of failure. The former, as we're about to see, can be solved with an afternoon on Microsoft Excel, the latter can take years to unpick.

My hypothesis here is simple. I reckon that if we really want to change our careers, if we *really* want to find fulfilling work, we'll figure out the dosh. There's just no other option. There's no escaping the fact that career changes or business launches often involve pay cuts. These may be temporary, but they also might not be. And, given that, we have to ask ourselves a straightforward question: is being poorer a price worth paying for being happier?

If not, then that's fine. You do you, as they say. But in my case, if you offered me that deal – earning less in return for being content – then, without hesitation, I'd take it. In some ways, I already have.

I was never the richest of my friends, but, before I quit full-time employment to write books and talk about them, I wasn't the poorest either. Whether I was twiddling my thumbs at the bank or flogging adverts to unsuspecting marketers, I always earned quite well. And accordingly, I was always able to buy tickets to things, and go on city breaks, and splurge online. Nowadays, all of that's gone. Irritatingly, despite what J. K. Rowling's success might suggest, writing words and then talking about them isn't a cash cow. And, without question, I'm now easily the poorest of my pals. My 'take home' last year was a pinch above the London Living Wage (although I think the word 'living' is meant ironically?), and consequently my lifestyle has taken what horticulturalists would call a 'hard pruning'. Where once I chasséd around in new trainers and a £35 haircut, now the simple act of ordering an Uber or 'adding guac' makes me feel like Mr Monopoly.

Oddly, losing the material stuff hasn't really bothered me. I say 'oddly' because for years I obsessed over it. Buying stuff was the pay-off for being miserable all week. I'd spend my weekends biffing money on pointless stuff to fill the void and justify the job. 'I hate my career, but at least I've got a car,' I used to think.

Now my thinking has changed. As long as I have enough money to pay the bills, eat and occasionally take Cali for dinner, I'm sort of OK. Which isn't to say I don't get envious. To be clear, there are moments when I'm deeply, deeply envious of my careerist friends and their new sofas, and fancy coffee machines, and holidays to Venice. But mostly it's fine. Certainly if it stayed like this forever, I'd die happy. Which, by the way, is how I justify my choices. Because at some point I'm going to find myself in an uncomfortable NHS bed, staring at a strip-lit ceiling, waiting for the Grim Reaper. And in that moment I reckon I'll care more about having lived a happy, fulfilled life than a lucrative one.

Ideally, of course, it'll be both. I'd love for something to go terrifically well and for me to earn gazillions in the process. But if that doesn't happen, if things stay more or less as they are, then that'll be fine.

Curiously, I'm not alone in thinking like this. In fact, according to the Harvard Business Review, 90 per cent of Americans say they would give up a significant portion of their earnings in return for more meaningful work. I must admit I found that surprising. I thought that most people were of the 'grin and bear it', 'work for the weekend' mentality. But as it happens, given the option, nearly all of us would take fuller hearts over thicker wallets.

The question is, of course, how to do it. If your job move or business launch requires taking a pay cut – or no pay at all – how do you live and get through that? You've decided that earning less is a price worth paying for feeling fulfilled, now what?

The answer depends slightly on the move you're making. If it's a straightforward switch from one type of full-time employment to another – say, from being an accountant to being a teacher – then mostly your battles will be psychological. It's depressing that teachers earn less than accountants, but it's also inescapable and you'll just have to get used to it. Your lifestyle will need a trim, you'll likely have to say 'no' to things. Accept this, surrender to it. You're making an active choice – *it's your decision* – to earn less. And you're making this compromise in order to be happier. Having a lower income is just the other side of the bargain – it's the irritating yin, to an otherwise wonderful yang.

If your plan is anything other than gainful employment – launching a business, for example – then things are a little more complex. Not impossible, just demanding of deeper thought. Or rather, deeper planning, parameters, flexibility and humility.

The first step is to decide your 'minimum liveable income' – the amount of money you need in order to live the most basic lifestyle you (and your dependants) are willing to accept. For some people, this will be the absolute minimum – just enough to live, eat and clothe oneself. For others, it'll be fractionally more lavish. Maybe there's a gym membership in there or the occasional dinner out. Either way, this is the only number that matters; this is your Holy Grail, your North Star – or whichever cliché you prefer. And once you've decided it, all you need is a plan to reach it. Which is where the flexibility and humility come in, because hitting your minimum liveable income will likely involve a variety of smaller, often lower status, and occasionally bizarre income streams.

Recently I've just about scraped by with the writing and talking thing, but in pursuit of my 'number', I've done all manner of part-time, sometimes wacky, gigs. I've waited tables, tutored children, sold Microsoft Excel training courses (or tried to). For a while I even carved out a niche doing voiceovers for tourist audio guides. God that was great work: £250 a day to sit in a sound booth, looking at pictures on an iPad and chatting rubbish. 'Legend has it . . .', I'd start before ad-libbing an anecdote about brutalist architecture or the Plantagenets, or both.

It's also important to remember that you don't have to transition from single to multiple incomes overnight. You can build up to it by introducing a weekend job here, a side hustle there (much more on these later), and only chuck in the towel with your employer once you're confident of reaching your 'minimum liveable'. This might take time and, for a while at least, it can make for a very hectic sched-ule. But if, like me, you're risk-averse, or scared of life with less money, it's a good way to go. I was about halfway through writing my first book – publishing deal in hand – before I felt comfortable handing in my notice. I just wanted to be totally sure that I could make it work, so I spent a good six months sniffing around part-time opportunities and income streams to give myself comfort that it was doable. Monday through to Friday I'd be poncing around the City flogging adverts, then on Saturday I'd be tutoring maths or donning my apron for a 'Bottomless Brunch' shift at a restaurant in Clapham. Wow, that was tough – three hours of serving 'unlimited booze' to a screeching throng of netball teams and hen dos, followed by three hours of clean-ing up the resulting puke. 'At least I'm getting paid,' I told myself as I mopped up my third pile of half-digested eggs

Benedict, still fizzing with the morning's Prosecco. 'It's good to know I've got options.'

But as well as planning how to hit your minimum liveable income – your Plan A – it's also important to consider what will happen if you don't or can't. What's your Plan B? Or Plan Bs, seeing as there are many potential routes out of failure. If the coffee shop goes bust or the part-time book-keeping job you had lined up disappears, what's your next move, or set of moves? And then what's your Plan Z? What are you going to do if, even after activating multiple Plan Bs, everything still goes tits-up, your business is a flop and you can't cobble together an income from working part-time? What are you going to do then? And, most importantly of all, how will you know when it's time to pull the ripcord and activate Plan Z? What are your critical success factors – the things that'll tell you you're headed in the right direction and should carry on? And what are your critical failure factors – the things that tell you it's over?

LinkedIn founder and serial entrepreneur Reid Hoffman calls this approach to career switches 'ABZ Planning'. And it's something that I found very helpful in plotting my path out of advertising. My Plan A, obviously, was to make a living writing and talking. In the dream scenario, that would have happened overnight, but, for obvious reasons, that was never particularly likely. So almost immediately I ended up turning to my Plan Bs. Importantly, these didn't represent different ends, just different means of reaching the original end. The destination – making a living from writing – stayed the same; the Plan Bs just meant different, more circuitous routes to getting there. At times, these winding paths felt very indirect indeed. 'I wonder if Hemingway ever did tele-sales?' I thought to myself while pitching to my fifth regional accountancy firm of the day. But have faith. Plan Bs are an essential part of getting to Plan A. And I'd recommend having lots of them up your sleeve – more than you think you'll ever need – just in case.

Which brings me to Plan Z. This is your absolute worst, *worst*-case scenario. It's what you'll do if, even after activating your Plan Bs, you're still stuck. Either you're not progressing at all towards Plan A, or you're doing so too slowly, or you've made a big bet which clearly hasn't paid off. Perhaps you launched a restaurant on the eve of the coronavirus pandemic or joined a charity on the day it got busted for embezzle-ment. At this point you need a plan which will enable you to survive and to rebuild. For me, as for lots of folks, this involved moving home and trying to get a job back in my old industry. And I pledged that I'd do this if, after two years of trying, I still couldn't live sustainably from writing. Or if my savings dipped below two months' worth of rent. Those were my two, cast-iron, 'critical failure' factors. If either of those things happened, the game was up – no ifs, no 'but I'm nearly there's.

Your plan and 'failure factors' might look very different to mine. Sadly, not everyone has the option of moving home to regroup. But that's OK. As we'll explore shortly, you don't have to make the transition in one leap. If you need slower, smaller increments in order to minimise risk and avert catastrophe, then be my guest. Just be sure to make the plans. Not only because they increase the likelihood of success, but also because they reduce our anxiety about failure. In a way we're doing what Vince did in Afghanistan. We're sizing up the challenge, prodding and poking it until it's reduced to a series of uncontrollable, hopefully un-worry-about-able probabilities. And that has to be good for our nerves.

But perhaps most importantly, having a plan increases the likelihood that you'll get going. The research here is very clear. The more we plan, the more likely we are to get off our arses and start moving towards our futures. Or, as researchers at New York University put it (in their wonderfully American way), 'forming an implementation intention' is highly 'effective in promoting the initiation of goal striving'.

It's difficult to overstate how important this is. As we saw earlier, the biggest blocker to career moves or business launches is inertia. It could be because we fear failure, or earning less money, or having less status. But often, if we're really honest, it's because we're lazy. The 'do nothing' option is always lower effort than 'do something', let alone the 'do something risky which might involve a pay cut or reduction in status'. And faced with that choice – between the effortless and the effortful – many of us default to idleness, even if doing so makes us miserable. In helping us to overcome this natural temptation, planning can be a hugely important piece in the career change puzzle.

Crucially, though, it must never become the whole puzzle. I'm stretching the metaphor (as per), but it's important that planning doesn't become procrastination. Making spreadsheets, writing lists and googling stuff might feel like progress, but there comes a point where 'analysis paralysis' creeps in and you find yourself researching and planning as ends, rather than means. Be alive to this danger and, when it happens, take it as your cue for action. If you remember the fable, you want to be the cat that dodges the marauding dogs by committing to a single escape plan, rather than the fox that has lots of plans but doesn't commit and subsequently gets torn limb from limb. After all, as Facebook supremo Sheryl Sandberg likes to say, 'done is better than perfect'.

Having made my plans, the next step was to share them with other people. This was handy because saying it all out loud allowed me to sense-check my thinking and build confidence. And, in a way, it also helped me to convince myself that I wasn't being rash or profligate. It helped me prove the validity of it all to myself.

Interestingly, the consensus about sharing our plans is a bit mixed. Until recently, most people felt that telling others about our intentions was a good thing. The theory being that, once you've told someone that you plan to quit smoking or lose weight, you'd be embarrassed into action. But nowadays researchers aren't so sure. Indeed, some psychologists, like Derek Sivers, believe that sharing our plans can in fact reduce the likelihood of us following through with them. 'When you tell someone your goal and they acknowledge it . . . the mind is kind of tricked into feeling that it's already done,' says Sivers. 'And then, because you've felt that satisfaction, you're less motivated to do the actual hard work necessary.' Huh.

But regardless of whether you share your plans (and my advice is that you do), the important thing is to make them in the first place. First establish how much dosh you need, then work out a panoply of plans to earn it (recognising that these plans will demand flexibility and humility), then decide on an escape route, your Plan Z, and then, finally, do it.

As I mentioned earlier, from start to finish the financial planning process took me about a year – six months of planning, six months of toe-dipping and then I jumped. You might get it done much quicker or it could end up taking twice as long. Either way, you will get there.

FEAR OF LETTING DOWN OTHERS

Other people play a huge role in our career choices. Without exception, every move I've made has been executed with an eye to other people's opinions. Or at least, my *perception* of other people's opinions. In reality, of course, only my closest mates give a monkey's what I do for money. But, when you're on the precipice of a big change or decision, you feel the piercing gaze of friends and family very keenly indeed. 'What's he done that for?' you imagine them saying. 'Why's she throwing it all away?'

But it's not just other people's opinions that we fear; sometimes, more subtly perhaps, it's the idea of letting people down which stops us from pursuing our futures. Most often, this fear is financial. As we just saw, career moves and finding fulfilling work often involves earning less. Which is kind of OK if it's just you, but what if it isn't? What if the question isn't simply 'is being poorer a price worth paying to make me happy?' and is instead 'is it OK to make my family poorer, too?'. It's one thing to pursue fulfilling work at your own expense, but quite another to do so to the detriment of your partner's lifestyle, your children's schooling or your parents' care.

Then there are the non-financial dependants. Perhaps you admire your boss or like your colleagues and worry that your departure would drop them in it. I had this exact conversation recently with a doctor friend. After nearly 10 years of studying, training, long hours and little money she's finally reached the point where she wants out. But, even though she's grown to despise the work, she feels unable to leave. 'We're so under-resourced,' she said. 'I can't leave because I know what that'll mean for the others.'

Obviously the self-sacrifice and altruism of the medical profession is exceptional. But you don't have to be an over-stretched junior doctor to worry what your move might mean for others. Even in my old industry of advertising sales – hardly renowned for its compassion or integrity – almost every leaving speech came dripping with guilt and apology. 'I'm so sorry to be leaving this close to bonus time,' I remember my colleague Chris saying. 'Hopefully you guys can make up the revenue somehow and still hit your target.'

But even if you don't have kids, or a partner, or nice colleagues, or a kind boss, there are still people who you might be nervous to disappoint. For me, unquestionably, the biggest were my parents. Not that they're pushy or easily disappointed. In fact, quite the opposite is true – they're warm, generous and supportive. Which is precisely why I've worried so much throughout my life about letting them down – be it at school, in sports or in my career.

And from my conversations with others, it seems that this is a common sentiment. In fact, pretty much everyone has expressed it in some form or another. Shakira's mum wanted her to be a property developer. Mae's dad thought she'd be an architect (like him). Hamid's dad hoped he'd join the family business, and so on. 'It's that whole thing of "I'm not angry, I'm just disappointed",' Camille (a Marketing Manager in recruitment) told me. 'Both my parents are teachers, and they were gutted when I didn't want to do the same.'

The first step in overcoming this complex dilemma is to realise that those closest to us will almost always have our best interests at heart. Of course they do. Of course they want us to be happy and fulfilled. The reason Shakira's mum wanted her to be a property developer, or why Mae's dad thought she'd be an architect, wasn't because they wanted their kids to be miserable. No, they pushed those careers because they thought they'd make them cheerful – either directly through the job itself or indirectly through the financial security and lifestyle the job would enable.

The challenge is then to unpick this and help those around us understand what we want from work. And, where necessary, to make them realise that what we want and what they want might be very different things. This involves some sales. Not much, thankfully. But you should spend some time considering your pitch and working out your 'why'. This is a slightly woolly concept, but you can think of it as your core motivation or purpose in life.

> Your 'why' is what makes you tick, what gets you out of bed in the morning, what fires you up about a working day.

It could be about learning new skills, or helping others, or earning loads of dosh. Or it might be about having time for your hobbies or making just enough to support the kids. Whatever it is, moving towards your 'why' is the central argument for why you're changing careers. And it's also almost impossible to argue with.

When, for example, I first started telling people of my intentions to quit advertising and try something new, the vast majority of my friends and family were bemused. Almost every conversation started with a Roger Moore eyebrow and something akin to 'but don't you have a fancy title and a decent pay packet?'. Sort of, I'd say. But the pursuit of those things was also making me desperately sad. It made me feel empty, and trapped, and useless. And I wasn't any good at it. There were some things in life I was quite good at, but my job involved none of them. Which only served to make me feel more useless, more lost.

Then I'd launch into my why.

I'd tell them how I craved creativity and autonomy. I'd explain how absorbing and soothing I found learning, how reading and researching quietened the noise in my head. 'I've been thinking about writing,' I'd say, sounding like the foppish lead in a noughties romcom. If that meant dropping down the income ladder, then so be it. I'd rather enjoy my work and earn less than be rich but suicidal. 'Fair enough,' they'd say after a few minutes. 'If you think that'll make you happy then you should do it.'

The obvious question is, 'Why bother?' Why take the time to convince those around you that your plans are good? Why not just do what you want? To hell with what other people think.

In part, I agree. As we saw earlier, most of us spend far, far too much time caring about what other people think. We allow their judgements (or our perception of their judgements) to influence everything, from how we dress and who we love to what we do and where we work. All of which are bad things that we should resist at all costs. And yet, with your closest friends and family it's different. Not only is it impractical to ignore what they think, it's also unhelpful. Making a career change is always going to be tough, but it's going to be so, so much harder if those closest to you (your parents, siblings, partner) think it's a rubbish idea. And while selling them on your ideal job might be momentarily uncomfortable, settling for a job you hate or trudging through a career pivot without their support will be a far worse affliction.

Looking back, I think I was too overconfident in these conversations. I did too much telling and not enough asking.

And if I could do it again, I'd be more honest about not having all the answers. Whether it was chatting to my parents or Cali, I wanted to project an image of having worked everything out. Which, according to the research, is not the best approach. Indeed, according to scientists like Professor Paul Zak, the way to garner someone's trust isn't to be overly confident, but to share your vulnerabilities. Apparently, sharing your weaknesses with someone stimulates the release of a hormone called 'oxytocin' in their brains which increases emotions like cooperation and trust.

And that's important.

When you're paddling out of career creek, you want as many people in your canoe as possible. You don't want your friends and family perched on the riverbank passively observing. You want them next to you, oar in hand, rowing like crazy to help you get there. So invite them to come aboard, hand them a paddle. Be thoughtful about what you want from work, and then communicate it honestly – worries, warts and all. If you do this, I promise you'll be astounded by how brilliant humans are. Even the ones you might be doubtful of. No, *especially* the ones you might be doubtful of.

Throughout all my recent turmoil – breaking down, living with anxiety, lurching from one career crisis to another – other humans have been my answer. Not totally – I've also had to potter and graft away alone, and sometimes not without prompting. But, occasionally, you have to be explicit, you have to say it out loud: 'Please help me.' And when you do, you'll be surprised by how much people will.

OVERCOMING CAREER FEAR

The fear	The problem	The remedy
Fear of failure	What if I switch careers or start my own thing and it all goes pear shaped?	Decide what you can control and what you can't – obsess about the former, and try to ignore the latter. Failing is crap; but not trying is even worse.
Fear of losing your identity	'I hate being an engineer, but if I'm not an engineer what am I?'	Accept that, whilst changing your career might involve leaving a part of your identity behind, it was a part of your identity that was unfulfilled and unhappy.
Fear of earning less	How can I make ends meet whilst transitioning careers?	Decide on your 'minimum livable income', develop your Plans A to Z, decide your critical failure factors and then get cracking. You don't have to move at 100 miles per hour. But you do have to move.
Fear of letting others down	What if changing jobs goes against my parents' / friends' / colleagues' expectations for my career?	Bring people with you by working out your 'why' and pitching / discussing it with them.

WHAT JOB SHOULD I DO?

HAVING SPENT THE past four chapters trying to convince you that fulfilling work is possible and that you should commit to discovering it, it's now time to address the two-ton, sequined elephant standing over there in the corner: *what job will I find fulfilling?*

This is the big one, the one on which so much depends. And yet it's also a question that, arriving into adulthood, most of us are shockingly ill-equipped to answer. It isn't our fault. The pace and structure of modern society do little to encourage youthful introspection and self-discovery, while our education system almost entirely ignores the question of what motivates us in life, what bores us and how we might like to spend our 85 or so years on earth. When most of us leave school aged 16 or 18 we haven't the faintest waft of what job we might enjoy. We can remember the name of Hitler's dog, sure. And the equation for photosynthesis. And the magnitude of the Kobe earthquake (7.2, I think). But ask us what careers we'd like and most of us will shrug, 'Erm, dunno . . . pilot?'

At my school, 'career advice' came in two stages. First you had a 30-minute conversation with a careers adviser the the school brought in for the day, then you did a multiple choice test thing.

The careers adviser I got was a misanthropic former Geography teacher with a cheap suit, furrowed brow and truly terrible halitosis. I mean it. Chatting with him was the conversational equivalent of cycling behind a rubbish truck – a proper, eye-watering, nostril-stinging assault on the senses. And the only thing worse than his breath was his career advice. Some of it was hilariously, eccentrically cynical. Some of it was mildly offensive. All of it was entirely pointless. 'You're far too tall for the civil service,' he told my friend Amir. 'No one will trust a teacher without glasses,' he told Lawrence. 'Aren't consultants supposed to be intelligent?' he said to Niall.

My own conversation with him lasted just 15 minutes on account of his needing the loo. 'Have you considered Law?' he asked, glancing at his watch. 'I doubt you'd get into a Magic Circle firm, though Slaughter & May might have you. And if not, something in the regions maybe. Ashurst or Macfarlanes. OK? Done? Good. Great. Must dash.'

Then I took the test, or 'tests' because there were four of them. It took a whole morning to do the bloody things and then there was a two-month wait for the results. The answer? Well, actually, there were two: either I was going to be a prison drama teacher (oddly specific, I know) or something called a 'lumber salesman'. Either I would be putting violent thugs through productions of *Oklahoma!* or selling wood to builders. Every single person I've spoken to who did one of these tests got similarly strange suggestions: Gemma (now a content marketing manager) was supposed to be a dog groomer; Mason (a graphic designer) should have been a submariner; Piotr (a structural engineer) was destined to be a speech therapist; and so on.

The silliness of these tests is both mildly amusing and not at all surprising (after all, most of them were developed in the mid-twentieth century, before most modern jobs existed). But the fact that, for lots of us, they comprise the full extent of our career enquiries also makes them problematic. If they were just one of a few things we did to identify our futures, then maybe they'd be a bit of gentle fun. But they aren't. They don't complement the hard thinking, they replace it. And as such, in taking these asinine tests, all we're doing is kicking the career can yet further down the road.

Often the plan is to work out what we want after leaving school. But, again, when does that ever really happen? Aren't we all too busy spending our late teens and early twenties drinking Glen's Vodka and trying to snog Gillian Walsh to uncover our profession? Maybe your education gives you some inkling of what you might like to do, but mostly you'll bumble along for a while, panic and then take the first gig you can get your hands on.

All of this is further complicated by the fact that many of us arrive at the question of our careers having been raised on a diet of meaningless – often misplaced – platitudes: 'Follow your heart,' we're told; 'Listen to your gut.' Both of which are dreadful ideas. Primarily because, as we saw earlier, the human 'heart' is terrible at guessing what makes us happy.

It's also scatty and inconsistent. Writing this at 10am I feel certain that I'd enjoy pasta for dinner tonight. Ask me in five hours, though, and doubtless it'll be tacos, or curry, or pizza. And it's the same with jobs. One day our gut tells us to quit accounting and be a singer, the next it thinks maybe plumbing is our true calling, and by the third, it's thinking that maybe accounting isn't so bad after all.

Which isn't to say that intuition is unhelpful – far from it. The human ability to synthesise information and make snap judgements is another of our evolutionary superpowers. But it's also a superpower that needs to be harnessed with logic, evidence and analysis. If we're to avoid lurching from one ill-fitting career to the next, we must, to borrow from Daniel Kahneman, 'think slow' as well as fast. Our hearts must work in unison with our heads, or else we're certain to follow the wrong paths.

We must also recognise that uncovering what we want from work will take time and require deliberate, effortful contemplation. It isn't just going to hit us one day. We're not going to wake up one morning with a fully formed idea of our ideal careers. A white-haired, wispy-bearded man isn't going to appear in the sky and boom, 'Your true destiny is to be a Social Media Manager, EMEA.'

It just doesn't work like that. And why would it? Discovering how we want to spend our working lives is one of the greatest questions we face as humans. And accordingly, it's reasonable to expect that the answer will involve sitting in a chair, or lying on a bed, or standing in the shower, and thinking really, really hard.

PHASE 1: THE LISTS

The road towards discovering your ideal career begins with a pen and paper (or the 'notes' section of your phone). You're going to – as I did – make two lists. One is a list of things you love in life, the other a list of things you despise. What are the things, the activities or engagements that get you most excited in life? And which have you rolling your eyes about and trying to think of excuses not to do? Not in work, in life. Which is a harder, broader question. But here broad is good. Because there's a strong chance – a very strong chance – that the career you'll end up loving is one which up until now you hadn't even considered or didn't know existed. And you're not going to be able to identify it while still using your old terms of reference. So, rather than writing 'Adobe Photoshop' on your list of likes, put 'creativity' or 'creating with technology'. Instead of putting 'meetings' on your dislikes, write 'routine' or 'talking rather than doing'. The aim is to really get to the bottom of what drives and motivates you in life, so, wherever you can, go deeper and broader.

Writing these lists properly takes time and requires effort. It's also much harder than you think. Particularly the 'dislikes' one, which is quite a negative, slightly uncomfortable process, as well as being quite navel-gazey and self-important. But working out what you dislike in life is really important because enjoyment isn't just the presence of pleasure; it's the absence of irritation, too. And in searching for a fulfilling, joyful career we must find one which maximises the good stuff while simultaneously minimising the bad. It would no good, for example, taking a job as an air steward because you love travel, only to discover that it involves lots of teamwork, which you hate. Better to be a travel writer, or risk analyst, or spy.

As you ponder and write your lists, try to be aware of two booby traps that society has cunningly laid for us.

The first relates to the wealth of totally unfounded, utterly false dichotomies which have somehow become accepted wisdom. I'm talking here about the notion that we must *either* be good at maths *or* good at arts. Either we're extroverts or introverts. Either we're driven by money or altruism. Either we're good at ideas or delivery. And so on. All of these ideas are just wrong. Of course they are. Of course it's possible to be both mathematically and artistically minded. How else would we have architects? Of course it's possible – no, entirely probable – that all of us have moments of both extroversion and introversion. Of course you can be into money *and* helping others. How else would philanthropy and foundations exist? And of course it's possible to be both good at ideas and good at seeing them through. Every business on earth was once an idea that someone delivered into reality (often alone).

Remember all this as you make your lists.

Don't allow society's contrivances to constrain your desires or guide your thinking.

Contradiction – or supposed contradiction – is central to being human. The combination of seemingly disparate, opposing qualities is what makes us so interesting to chat to, so fascinating to fall in love with. Embrace this idea as you write your lists. Try to distil what you want, what you love and hate, not what society has told you.

The second bear trap is the idea that our true calling can be uncovered by regressing back to our childhoods. 'What were your earliest memories of enjoyment?' career counsellors ask. 'What classes did you most enjoy at school?', 'What did you want to be when you grew up?'

At first glance, thinking like this seems intuitive. Casting our minds back to the still, quiet innocence of youth – back to a time before our passions were corrupted by the demands of adulthood and poisoned with the cynicism of experience – makes sense. Grown-up life, with its responsibilities and social pressures, has the potential to cloud our judgement. It's infinitely busier, more frantic, more chaotic than our childhoods. And in this clattering, rowdy environment it's trickier to decipher the signals from the noise. Am I really motivated by money or do I just have a mortgage to pay? Do I really enjoy teamwork or do I just say that to get a promotion? Going back to a time before all that should, in theory, make our enquiries more accurate. It'll ground our 'likes' and 'dislikes' lists in our oldest, most pronounced passions.

And yet, for me at least, it was an almost entirely pointless process. Largely because – obvious point here – I'm an entirely different person today than when I was eight. Back then, my primary passions were eating toast, bouncing on a trampoline and amassing a vast (and, I maintain, very impressive) collection of Beanie Babies. Even the most earnest of child psychologists would struggle to divine a greater meaning from my childhood interests. I was a child, interested in childish things, doing childish things. And while a trip down memory lane is always fun, the idea that it might help me uncover my future was – swear word here – bullshit. Just as I wouldn't trust my eight-year-old self to pick my pension provider or drive me to the airport, I don't trust him to choose my career, either.

Others disagree. One person in particular I spoke to (now a very happy product designer) was convinced that his child-hood love of Meccano predicted his adult career. 'It was a sign,' he said. 'Of all the Christmas presents, the Meccano was the one I was most drawn to. Since then, I've always been drawn to make things.' Fair enough, I thought, sounds convincing. But then again, I also loved Meccano and I haven't the faintest interest in designing products. And neither do my two brothers, or my best friend Charlie, or my cousin Amy, all of whom were obsessed with those little strips of metal. So how does that work?

It took me two weeks to write my lists. I did it on trains, and on buses, and on the loo. Whenever I had a few spare moments or a passive flash of inspiration I'd whip out my iPhone and jot it down, taking time every few days to consolidate it all. And periodically I'd chat through my ideas with Cali or with close friends. I don't propose punting your lists around too widely, but the considered, objective counsel of a chosen few can be very helpful.

In total, I had four big likes and two massive dislikes. Learning new things, social interaction, an element of creativity and showing off a bit were the pluses. While the minuses were routine and working with pessimists. Wherever I've encountered the former in life, I've felt content and enthused. Wherever it's been the latter, I've been lost and bored. All of which is fairly self-explanatory. And, thankfully, all itches which I can scratch by writing a bit, speaking a bit and side hustling a bit. Even before making my lists, I had an inkling that that was what I wanted from my career. But going through the process, doing the thinking and having the conversations were still hugely instructive.

PHASE 2: READING JOB DESCRIPTIONS

Having made your lists you'll have a strong, written-down idea of what motivates and bores you in life. The aim now is to match those core pleasures and pains to potential roles and industries. There are a few possible ways to undertake this coupling exercise, but the thing I found most helpful was reading lots and lots of job descriptions.

I read ones I thought I'd be into, ones I thought I'd be totally wrong for and, above all, I sought out ones that I'd never heard of. And while I read, I tried to estimate the extent to which each gig was married with my 'likes' and divorced from my 'dislikes'.

Life as a Criminal Case Worker would have involved learning lots (good), interacting with others (great) and maybe a pinch of showing off (best of all). But there wouldn't be much creativity, and doubtless there'd be plenty of pessimists. Working as a Researcher at the British Library, in contrast, would likely involve lots of passionate, enthusiastic co-workers. But would there be much creativity? Marketing Manager for a financial technology start-up definitely would. Plus there'd be plenty of social interaction and, given that it's a start-up, less routine than usual. But at the same time, would I really be learning that much?

On and on I went, chomping through the job descriptions on Indeed.com. The trick is to set some very loose parameters ('London, full-time, £35k per annum'), and then dive in, saving or screenshotting anything which takes your fancy. The objective isn't so much to find jobs which you can apply for there and then. It's more about building a bank of ideas which you can use to focus your search later on. It's about finding roles you never knew existed and industries you'd never thought of. And, as long as you're able to approach it with a spirit of total open-mindedness, it's both liberating and huge fun.

It also taught me two important lessons.

The first was just how easily I'm blinded by a sexy title or industry. This was a big problem for me, and my guess is that it will be for you, too. Presented with an advert for an 8 out of 10 role in an unsexy industry (e.g. waste management) or a 2 out of 10 in a sexy one (e.g. restaurants), I almost always clicked on the latter. And the same was true of the employer's brand – a role at Heineken or Nike was always more enticing than one at Boring Co. or Blah Industries, even if the job itself was a terrible match.

It also taught me that you can find very similar 'likes' and 'dislikes' in seemingly very different roles. And as such it's unwise to write off jobs based solely on their titles. Not always, obviously. Once you've read one 'Store Manager' job description and decided it wasn't for you, you needn't read any more. But I was amazed by how often I'd start reading a job description expecting a total mismatch, only to discover that, on deeper interrogation, it was actually a reasonable fit.

If, for example, you enjoy educating others and helping people solve problems, the obvious career choice would be teaching. But from spending a few days reading job descriptions you might just as easily become a management consultant or even a salesperson. Those roles also involve education and problem-solving; and if money is on your 'likes' list, they might even be better fits than teaching.

Of course, there's also a possibility that – even after making your lists and studying the job descriptions – you're still left with a niggling doubt that you'd rather do your own thing. That could mean launching a business, going freelance or a hodgepodge of the two. That's where I got to; and if it's the same for you, then great. But if it isn't – if you'd rather work for someone else (or if you need the security of doing so) – that's equally valid.

I say this because, for some reason, we often fetishise entrepreneurship. Books about jobs almost inevitably lead to the suggestion that you should quit working for the man and go it alone. Politicians are always harping on about small businesses being 'the lifeblood of the economy'. And they are. But so are the people who work for the small businesses, and the medium and big ones. Yes, our economy needs a steady supply of people daring enough to start their own PR firm, restaurant or clothing line. But we also need lots of talented, dedicated and ambitious people to help them get there.

If starting your own business maximises your likes and minimises your dislikes, then absolutely you should do it. At the same time, though, you mustn't feel deflated or inadequate if, actually, you'd rather have a boss.

PHASE 3: GOING WITH IT

In making our lists and reading job descriptions, the aim is to uncover our deepest passions and pains, and to then marry them with roles and industries. The next step is to apply, interview and get the darned things (much, much more on this later). But before you do, it's crucial to remember this 18-carat, fully-guaranteed fact – no job will ever meet 100 per cent of your desires, 100 per cent of the time.

Sounds simple, I know. And it is. But it's also extremely important. Because, even if we spend ages diligently planning our futures, there are still going to be moments of panic and boredom. There are still going to be great weeks and crummy months. Moments of high pressure and pace, and moments of tedium. Days where we love what we do and days where, actually, we'd really rather stay in bed. And, above all, we must remember that we're never cured of wondering 'what if?': 'what if I hadn't quit being a sales-man?', 'what if I had made this move five years earlier?', 'what if I changed careers again?'

Asking 'what if?' is natural, and normal, and a key tenet of being alive. And sometimes we're going to conclude that we've made a mistake. 'What if?' will lead to 'I should have'. That's OK. Over the course of our careers, we are going to make mistakes. And what we want from life and from work is also bound to change, too. For most of us, this evolution-ary process is slow enough that only minor, incremental career adjustments are required. You might, for example, reach a point where you desire fewer learning opportunities for yourself and more responsibility to nurture others. That doesn't mean you need to quit banking or policing. It just means you need a managerial role. Or, conversely, perhaps you want less responsibility. Maybe you used to get a kick out of managing others, but would now prefer to do the work yourself. Fantastic. But, again, you don't need another wholesale career change; you need a conversation with your boss.

However, it may also be that, as you age, your 'likes' and 'dislikes' alter so fundamentally that you need to switch careers for a second or third time. That's also OK. Just go slow. Don't file for divorce the moment your partner starts snoring, no matter how tempting that may be. Instead, revisit your lists, reconsider what drives and bores you, and go again.

It's like that bit in Louis de Berniere's *Captain Corelli's Mandolin* (the bit which gets read at roughly 98 per cent of weddings) where the father counsels his daughter on what love is and isn't. 'Love is not breathlessness, it is not excitement, it is not the promulgation of promises of eternal passion. That is just being "in love",' he tells her. 'Love itself is what is left over when being in love has burned away.' It's the same with our jobs. Fulfilling, contented work isn't a fancy title, a company car or an employer your parents have heard of. It's waking up in the morning knowing that what you're about to do for the next eight hours aligns with what you love about life. It's knowing that the working day is going to enhance your existence, not detract from it. It's knowing, finally, that your life has meaning and purpose.

HOW SHOULD I DEFINE SUCCESS?

IT ISN'T THE cheeriest or easiest read, but if you're ever on the hunt for something existential/midlife crisis-y (no, just me?), I'd thoroughly recommend Leo Tolstoy's *A Confession*. Which isn't me pretending to have read lots of Tolstoy – I've never owned a copy of *War and Peace* and the closest I got to Anna Karenininina was that terrible movie with Kiera Knightley. But a clever friend recommended *A Confession* and, seeing as it's mercifully short, I gave it a go.

It's an elegant, erudite investigation into the meaning of life written at a time when its author was experiencing an existential meltdown of his own. When it was first published in 1882, Tolstoy was among the richest, most famous and most celebrated authors on earth. And yet, for all the dosh, celebrity and nice letters from Dostoyevsky and Chekov, he remained unfulfilled and unsure of his purpose on earth. 'I could give no reasonable meaning to any single action or to my whole life,' he writes. Worse, if the things that he thought would make him happy (money, fame, etc.) didn't, what would? 'Had a fairy come and offered to fulfil my desires,' he says, 'I should not have known what to ask.'

The prose that follows is both utterly beautiful and not entirely relevant for us. What matters for us isn't Tolstoy's answer to the question of why he exists, it's that he's asking it in the first place. Because by the usual definitions of success – money, fame, power – Tolstoy should be the happiest man in Russia. But he isn't. Instead, he's depressed, rueful, panicked. He's spent his whole life climbing a mountain only to discover that the view from the top is the same as the view from the bottom. Except it's actually a bit worse, because there's nowhere else to go. The illusion – that reaching the peak would fix him – is gone.

Naturally, Tolstoy isn't the first person to define success, achieve that definition and then discover that it was bullshit.

> For centuries people have been charging after fame, influence and wealth only to discover that attaining these things leaves them itchy and hollow.

And it isn't just celebs and famous writers who experience this phenomenon. Normal people, too, have the unsettling sensation of becoming rich and powerful, only to find that they're still miserable.

Recent research from the University of Rochester in New York found exactly this. The study (which asked college graduates to evaluate their life goals and happiness at one- and two-year intervals after graduation) found that the pursual of 'American Dream goals' (aka money, fame and power) 'does not contribute to happiness at all'. And that in actual fact 'it does contribute to some ill being'. Indeed, as one of the interviewees put it: 'The whole process of being so on the treadmill to wealth, fame and image leaves me feeling like a pawn or a puppet in life.'

And yet, if I offered you a slot on that treadmill, I'm willing to bet you'd take it. We all would. We don't seem to care what others say; we don't hear their words of warning. We see reality stars taking overdoses, and bankers jumping out of skyscrapers, and, still, we don't believe them. Still, we obsess over cash, power and fame. 'I reckon it'd be different if it was me,' we say to ourselves.

Of course, the corrupting, hollowing influence of money and celebrity isn't universal. Some people do get out alive; many enjoy it all a great deal. ('I love being famous!' said actor Will Smith recently. And I'm sure he does.) My only point is that lots of people don't. Lots of us – me included – feel perplexed, lost and excluded by the traditional definition of success. We're not that into money, or amassing influence, or celebrity, or a million Instagram followers; and as such, 'success', as viewed by modern society, isn't really available to us.

At the same time, though, definitions of success which eschew money completely also don't feel right. 'Focus on finding your inner balance, not building your bank balance' et al, might look fantastic on a bumper sticker, but are they realistic, achievable approaches to life? Probably not. Unless you're going to go full nomad, your existence will demand a bank balance. And seeing as hippy-ish protestations aren't (yet) legal tender, you're going to have to focus some of your life on building that bank balance. You can't yoga your way out of the council tax or meditate the phone bill away.

But if success isn't necessarily money, fame and power, or inner peace and growth, then what on earth is it? What is it, how do we achieve it and, perhaps most importantly, how will we know when we have?

SUCCESS IS . . . PERSONAL

The first thing to say about success is that it's deeply, unshakably personal. It's biased, subjective and often illogical. What feels right for me might seem absurd to you, and vice versa. And as such there can be no such thing as a singular, universal definition. Instead, the best we can do is develop a framework through which we can define our version of success.

Doubtless you've already spent some time thinking about what that might look like. I certainly have. Even before embarking on this book, I was oddly obsessed with trying to understand success. Or rather, obsessed with trying to define what it meant for me and panicking that I wasn't moving towards it. Along with what to have for breakfast and the success of other authors, it remains one of the top three things I think about in the shower.

Acknowledging that success is personal – that your definition will differ from your friends' or parents' – is freeing. It allows you to stop feeling embarrassed that you don't want what others do, or do want what others don't. In other words, it allows you to pursue the life and career you desire; one that's personal and perfect for you, rather than one foisted on you by others.

One of the reasons that we panic and agonise so much over success is that we rarely discuss it. We're cagey about our life goals and our thoughts on success, because how you define success seems to say so much about you as a person. To admit that you want to be richer than God or Elon Musk (at the time of writing they're roughly equal) is to suggest you're shallow and materialistic. To say that success lies in helping others is to signal your virtue, to hint at your hidden depth. And so on.

Acknowledging that success is personal does away with all this stigma. It helps us to realise that my definition isn't better or more profound than yours; it's simply different. And just as you don't jump to conclusions based on who someone fancies, or their hair colour, or their favourite pasta sauce, we shouldn't judge people for their definitions of success.

Your definition of success is yours and yours alone. And you must never feel embarrassed or ashamed by it.

SUCCESS IS . . . MORE THAN WORK

This might seem an obvious point, but doing well at work and being successful are not necessarily the same thing. They are closely interwoven, sure, but it's also perfectly possible to be riotously high-performing at work and still not see your-self as successful or, as has become clear, to feel happy and fulfilled.

In part, that's because our traditional definitions are intangible and ever-expanding. How big of a bonus is enough to say you're successful? How many times must you be promoted? How many direct reports do you need? On all counts, the answer is usually an elusive 'more'.

There's also an issue of relativity. When you're a trainee you derive your definition by looking at other trainees, whereas once you're a Partner you're comparing yourself to other Partners. How you see success shifts – quietly, unknow-ingly – as you get older. Meaning that, even though you might have smashed the goals you set aged 20, you're still restless at 30.

But the main reason why professional performance and success aren't necessarily tied is because there is just more to existence than work. Work, careers, how we spend our days are hugely important facets of existence, but they're not the only ones. Forming meaningful friendships, falling in love, learning, travelling . . . most of life's great moments exist outside of the workplace. And accordingly, while work is unquestionably an important part of how we define success for ourselves, it can never be the entirety.

SUCCESS IS . . . A SERIES OF MOMENTS

It's tempting to think of success as a singular thing, a moment in time, a destination, an end. That's what we're taught growing up. Someone is either successful or not; they either have 'it' or they don't.

In reality, though, success is more fractured and nebulous, bitty and temporal. There's no one moment or metric that will tell you you've 'completed' your definition of success. Instead, there will be many, many events, emotions and achievements which, combined over time, will make you feel successful.

To my mind, we can break these 'moments' down into three broad categories – let's call them nano, micro and macro.

Nano successes are things like making your bed, being early and meeting deadlines. They're everyday rituals, done well; and they're essential to any feelings of success. It doesn't matter how much you earn or how grand your title is, if you come home to piles of dirty dishes or repeatedly forget your mother's birthday, you aren't going to feel successful.

Micro successes are bigger, more notable life events – once a year-ish things like getting a promotion, or pay rise, or passing an exam, or losing a certain amount of weight. It's difficult to overstate how important these kinds of successes are. They provide us with moments of real, shareable pride, but they also help us to keep momentum. They're the filling in the sandwich, the jam in the doughnut, the stake in the ground which says 'this year I achieved X, and that shows me I'm living up to my potential'.

Macro successes – the final category – are things like having children, selling your company, getting married, buying a home. These are the biggest, most photographable life events. And they're also central to how most of us define success. Too central, if you ask me. We spend far, far too much time obsessing over the macro moments, and not nearly enough on the micro and nano. We build these things up in our minds and make such a fuss about achieving them that, when we do, it often feels anticlimactic. We think that selling a business, or moving to the countryside, or having children is going to complete us. And if it doesn't – say because we still hate our jobs, or had a break-up, or haven't exercised for six months – we have a Tolstoyan moment of our own. 'This was supposed to complete me,' we think. 'Now that it hasn't, what do I do?'

I'm not suggesting that we should ignore macro successes entirely, but you have to agree that on their own they're not enough. Like the lottery winners from earlier, the buzz of the big moment fades over time. And without a strong supporting scaffold of micro and nano successes, the sensation of success crumbles.

SUCCESS IS . . . FULFILLING YOUR POTENTIAL

In recent months I've concluded that the times I feel successful are the times I feel I'm fulfilling my potential and trying my best.

It's not necessarily about *achieving* so much as it is about *trying*; about moving forward, however small those movements might be.

The outcomes – the nano, micro and macro successes – are an important way of keeping score. But my overall contentment, my satisfaction with my life and work, is about the effort I'm making, not the things where I can say I'm 'winning'.

It was a conversation with a vicar which brought me around to this way of thinking. The Reverend Jon Finch isn't your typical priest – he's a young, cool dude from Southampton who has one of the fastest growing congregations in the UK. I wanted to speak with him to understand how you define success when the normal modern definitions of success aren't available to you. Having signed up to be a man of the cloth, Jon has necessarily opted out of the pursuit of money, fame and power. If everything goes to plan, his life will never be one of material wealth, power or prowess. He'll never sell a business, or drive a flash car, or get a second home on the Costa del Sol. And there also isn't much room for career progression: 'It goes vicar, archdeacon, bishop, archbishop and then God,' Jon told me. 'So the maximum amount of promotions I could ever have would be three.'

It was in chatting to Jon that I landed on this idea of fulfilling your potential as success. 'I see success as discovering and growing into your unique potential as a human.' For him this means helping people to turn their lives around or, as he put it, 'helping people to get from A to B'. Jon feels as though, for whatever reason, he's better than most people at doing this. He has a gift for helping people – be it an alcoholic who needs to stop drinking, a thief who needs to quit stealing or a married couple going through a rough patch. And as long as he's exercising that gift, as long as he's fulfilling his potential, he considers his life to be successful.

I should say that I'm not at all religious, but even I can see how this approach to success is freeing. It means that success is open to all of us, it's universally possible, it's inclusive. You can be poor, powerless, unemployed or filthy rich and still be 'successful'. All of which makes total sense and is a tremendously good thing.

The problem, though, with an approach like this is that it's woolly, nebulous and unquantifiable. If success isn't earning 'X thousands of pounds a year' or having 'Y job title by the age of 30', then how can you know you've achieved it?

The answer – and I promise this isn't a cop-out – is that you'll just know. Once you stop thinking about success in terms of numbers and grand moments, and focus instead on fulfilling your potential, you'll very quickly develop a sense of when you are successful and when you're not. And, to be sure, there are lots of times when you won't be. In fact, in my experience, most days are unsuccessful ones. Perhaps I've been lazy, or missed deadlines, or half-arsed some writing. Or I could have been rude to someone, or short-tempered, or forgotten something important. On those days, no, I'm not successful. I haven't lived up to my potential. I haven't done my best. Better luck next time.

But at least I'm not chasing something I don't want. At least I'm not trying to squeeze or deny my aspirations in order to conform to other people's definitions of success. And at least, most importantly, it's all on me. Focusing on efforts and inputs, rather than outputs or achievements means that I'm on the hook. No one else is to blame if I'm not successful. With titles, money or power this isn't the case. These achievements are contingent to some extent on other people. There's luck involved in getting a promotion or extracting a monster bonus. With the 'fulfilling your potential approach', though, I'm the only person responsible. There's a temptation, of course, to use this as an excuse for inaction: 'No one will know if I don't try, so why bother?' If that's you, fair enough; but you do forfeit your right to moan, and grumble, and howl at the wind. Defining success in this way means that we're the only ones to blame for failure. And if you can harness that idea, it should be a huge, huge motivation.

DO I NEED A SIDE HUSTLE?

THE USUAL FORM when writing about side hustles (defined here as work or a project which earns you money in addition to your main job) is to trot out the same, tired stories of people who started little businesses in their spare time, but who – shock, horror – subsequently achieved monster success.

We could, for example, spend the next few pages poking around the story of Houzz – the home decoration website which began as a fun side project, but is now worth $4 billion. Or we might explore the Khan Academy, the online tutoring platform launched by its founder, Salman Khan, to teach his cousin maths, but which now boasts tens of millions of students. Or we could look at Spanx, which Sara Blakely founded while selling fax machines door-to-door, but which ultimately made her the world's youngest female billionaire. Even Apple – yes, Apple, the richest company in the world – was at one point a side hustle for Steve Jobs and his co-founder Steve Wozniak. In the late seventies, Jobs was working at Atari and Wozniak was at Hewlett Packard, but they'd meet after hours in Jobs's garage where they built their first ever computer, the Apple-1.

Obviously, all of these corporate smash hits are deserving of our praise and admiration. And yet, holding them up as the benchmark or inspiration for our own side ventures somehow misses the point. Because side hustles, most often, are meant to be just that. They're a bit on the side, a fun weekend indulgence, an after-hours project which allows us to commercialise a hobby or skill. We're trying to sell our pottery online, or teach Spanish, or run cookery classes, not build the world's largest tech multinational or a billion-dollar website. And pretending as though we are – or thinking that the only ambition worth having is one of huge success – is neither realistic nor helpful.

The history of side hustling is more or less the history of the Internet. The term itself is a bit older than that; it first started appearing in African-American newspapers like *The Chicago Defender* and *The Pittsburgh Courier* in the fifties, but it wasn't until the noughties that the idea of earning outside of your main job caught the public imagination.

It really all kicked off after the credit crunch. That was when, faced with an economic collapse, lots of us first started considering additional income streams. And it was also the moment when technology started to make it all possible. As public trust in websites like eBay, Craigslist, Etsy and Gumtree grew, and as payment platforms like PayPal made transactions with strangers less shady, more and more of us felt comfortable earning from our extracurriculars – whether that was crafting, or babysitting, or assembling someone's Ikea order. Now we could earn money without a boss and without having to formally launch a business.

Then came a second, even stronger, wave of tech advancement, and with it a new crop of more sophisticated side hustles. No longer was it simply a case of advertising yourself through various digital classified ads. Now, using sites like Wix, GoDaddy, Squarespace and, later, Shopify, you could create your own website, build your own brand and turn your hobby into a proper business. Suddenly, e-commerce and web design, once the preserve of a nerdy few in Silicon Valley, were now available to the masses.

For some, this meant a small but welcome additional outcome – a 'wallet warmer' as Del Boy would say. For others, it meant making millions, particularly for those who got involved in the (slightly dodgy) world of drop-shipping. That's where you find a cheap product for sale in China (garlic crushers, knock-off headphones), build a jazzy website to sell it (at a massive mark-up) and only order the products from China once you make a sale. Sounds simple and it is. But it's also – if you're good at it – extremely lucrative. One Uruguayan chap called Gabriel Beltran went from struggling to pay his rent and living off his girlfriend's student loan, to living in Miami and earning over £20 million a year by drop-shipping, amongst other things, fake NFL gear.

But beyond selling products, the tech revolution also allowed us to monetise our free time. Today, with just a few thumb taps, any of us can become a cabbie, or a delivery driver, or a property manager. And millions of us do – in the six years from 2013 to 2019, the amount of people working in the UK's 'gig economy' doubled to over 4.7 million workers. Naturally, not all of those are side hustlers – lots of folks nowadays gig as a full-time occupation – but many of them are. They're normal people – teachers, nurses, sales reps, receptionists – trying to bulk out their primary earnings with some little bits on the side.

Of course, there's a worthwhile and fiery debate to be had about the ethics and politics of the gig economy, but that's not what's most pressing for us. The most pertinent question here isn't 'should side hustles come with workers' rights?', it's 'should I get one and, if so, how?'

The first part of that question seems like an obvious home run – who doesn't want to earn £20 million a year and live in Miami? But in reality, it's quite a bit more nuanced than that. It all depends on where you're at with your primary career.

If you love your main profession and just want some extra weekend fun, then absolutely you should crack on. Or if, as we saw earlier, you're side hustling as a means of making money while changing careers, then that's great too. The problem, however, comes when you hate your primary job, but use side hustling as a distraction. Because in that circumstance, all you're doing is prolonging your misery and ducking the proper, hard-but-vital task of discovering a career you might love. It's like being in a failing relationship – a string of saucy, one-night stands with strangers might temporarily scratch the itch and allow you to limp on, but it isn't sustainable. At some point you'll have to do the difficult thing and break up, so why not get it out of the way now?

The point is, side hustles are supposed to be either long-term, sustainable, happy, joyful things that you do in addition to a main career you love. Or they're a means to an end while you transition careers. But they must never be band-aids for broken legs.

I speak from experience here. Throughout all the jobs I've hated – whether it was selling ads or dossing around banks – I always saw side hustles as a panacea, an escape slide out of the tedium. 'If I can just think of something fun to do alongside this career,' I thought, 'perhaps I can make myself comfortable enough to ride out the boredom.'

Over beers in our local, my mate Olly and I would spend hours brainstorming potential (read: terrible) business ideas. 'A food truck that only sells boiled eggs? No, a food truck that only sells toast? That could work. Who doesn't love toast? And I bet the margins are good. But we'd need a van and they're probably expensive. Hmm. What about tech? We could do something tech-y, like, erm, what about Facebook for business? Sort of LinkedIn, but with a twist? Maybe it's LinkedIn but totally anonymous? Would that work? I still quite like the toast idea. Wait, I've got it – an anonymous social network for business people who love toast?'

Most of our 'businesses' (thank God) didn't make it past the second beer, but some did. Olly's idea for a cut-price concierge service called 'Household Heroes', for example, sailed through our rigorous selection process and into trading (only to be wound up six months later following 'challenging economic conditions'). And, when I mentioned my ice cream boat idea back at the beginning, I wasn't joking. That was the other one that got quite far. I devoted at least three months to registering the domains, finding an ice cream supplier, getting permissions from the harbour master, and so on. To this day I maintain it could work, if only I can work out how to fit a freezer onto a rowing boat.

The ideas themselves may have differed wildly, but the life cycle of each one was the same. First came the 'holy shit this is a great idea' phase – a few weeks of sheer excitement, furious research and emailing. It's also when I'd start drunkenly pitching the idea to friends: 'I'm going to make millions out of this subscription toothpick business, you'll see!' All good fun, but also painfully fleeting. Because after a month or so I'd arrive at the second phase – 'perhaps this isn't a great idea after all'. Soon followed by the 'yep, that's the end of that' phase. Then I'd be back to the grind and drudgery of selling adverts. Back to mornings spent contemplating my pointlessness and afternoons wishing I was somewhere – anywhere – else.

My mistake was not realising that side hustles are supposed to be fun, enhancing additionals, not distractions from a main job you hate.

Side justles are vitamins to improve your professional life, not painkillers to numb it.

In launching X or Y thinking that it'd provide just enough fulfilment to keep me plodding through my main career which I hated, all I was doing was prolonging my suffering, dodging the real question and ducking the hard-yet-essential work of discovering what I actually wanted to do.

But if that doesn't apply to you – if you've arrived at, or are moving towards, a main career you enjoy – then absolutely you should consider side hustling. And the good news is that, as I mentioned above, it's never been easier to start something. With a few hundred quid you can register a domain, build a templated website and get going. So why wouldn't you launch your sportswear brand, or write articles, or sell wedding photography?

Plus, with the coming revolution in home working (and make no mistake, it *is* coming), more and more of us will have the flexibility to choose what we work on and when. Unshackled from the rigid confines of an office-based 9 to 5, we'll be able plan our days as we wish. We'll do our primary work emails in the morning, a bit of side hustling at 11ish, back to the main gig after lunch and then round off the day with a few extracurricular meetings.

The coronavirus pandemic did much to accelerate all of this. The number of homeworkers in 2020 was roughly double the 2019 levels. And beyond the practical constraints, it also forced us to turn an attitudinal corner, too. Where once, pre-corona, people were shy or embarrassed about sharing their side hustles, now it's much more accepted. Lockdowns, furlough and rocketing unemployment left many of us with no choice but to get creative with our careers. Chefs had to become cookery instructors, actors became tutors, cabin crew administered vaccines.

And beyond those who pivoted or launched businesses from necessity, there were thousands more who did so out of boredom. All those long, featureless weekends, which we'd previously spent boozing, brunching and seeing friends, became filled with commerce. People sold their paintings, did pottery and launched vlogs. Those who used to be embarrassed or cagey about their side hustles, now promoted their little businesses with glee. The squeamishness was gone. 'Who cares?' we said to ourselves. 'Nowadays everyone has their "thing" so why can't I?' Like Ayesha, a graphic designer, who used the pandemic to launch an online events business. Or Marc, a film producer, who started a charity providing free meals to NHS workers. Or Julia, who worked as a journalist before launching a lockdown grocery delivery service. 'We were in the middle of a pandemic,' she said, 'but I'm optimistic, single-minded and perhaps a bit naïve so thought, what the hell?'

All of this is, of course, welcome news. As we've seen repeatedly in this book, the biggest blockers to progress and personal development are always mental. In helping us to overcome these, the pandemic has given many of us a welcome kick up the chuff. It stripped away some of the psychological barriers to 'having a go' and encouraged entrepreneurship. It gave us the confidence – or the imperative – to believe in ourselves and our ideas, which is such an important component of fulfilment. 'The best ideas don't die in the marketplace, or in the laboratory, they die in the shower,' says businesswoman Linda Rottenberg. 'Because people don't even give themselves permission to walk out of the shower, and write it on a napkin, and take it into the world.' Now, though, they do. And if you feel like you've got a great idea or just a fun one – and you're happy in your primary career – then it would be remiss not to go for it.

My own personal side hustle might surprise you. I make kitchen knives. A little left field, I know. But when I was recovering from my breakdown a friend suggested getting into cooking for its absorbing, mindful and rewarding qualities. And she was right – taking the time to properly plan, prepare and cook a meal soon became one of the things I looked forward to most in my day (particularly in the evenings after a hard day hating work). So I did what all men do when they discover a new hobby, I started buying all the kit. And that was when I spotted a gap in the market for handmade knives that didn't cost the earth. So I raided my Help to Buy ISA, enlisted my mate Thomas and set about finding a blade maker and a carpenter. That's been the hardest part – making the things. Everything else has been relatively easy. We use Shopify for the website, Instagram for advertising, Cali, for graphic design (she keeps threatening to invoice me, but so far I've got away with it) and then I do all the postage and packaging.

It's huge, huge fun, primarily because it's so different to my full(ish)-time occupation. I adore researching, writing and speaking, but I also get a kick from chatting with customers who buy my knives and the other small business folks who supply us. Just last week I spent an hour with the guy who makes the little brass plaques for the table numbers in pubs. Sounds interminably dull, I know. But he's obsessive and his passion for plaques was oddly infectious. Plus he's made a load of cash, which is always intriguing: 'I put three kids through private school with those plaques,' he told me. 'And we've got a place in Spain.'

Realistically, I'm not sure that my knives will ever earn me a villa in Marbella, but that isn't really the point. It's not about getting rich, it's about indulging some interests which aren't currently being met by my primary career. If I can 'warm my wallet' while doing that, then that's wonderful. Mostly, though, my motivation is to introduce variety and additional enjoyment to my working life. It's something extra, a fun thing to turn to on the days when I'm not thrilled by 'the usual'. There's also something hugely gratifying and exciting about selling a product or service that wouldn't have existed without you. The 'order placed' notification emails are the ultimate nano successes – little bumps of adrenaline and pride to enhance your day.

PREPARING FOR LAUNCH

So, how do you do it? Well, first you'll need an idea. It could be a hobby that you're already passionate about, but it also doesn't have to be. You could have spotted a gap in an existing market. Or you could apply a new business model to an old industry. Or perhaps you just have an innate talent for something which might seem unremarkable to you, but which people are willing to pay for. My videographer friend Alex, for example, has carved out a side hustle helping people to write their wedding speeches. He's not a comedian or writer, but for whatever reason he's mastered the art of making mums cry and dads laugh. And people are happy to reward him handsomely for his services (about £300 for 1,000 words apparently). 'I don't necessarily love writing the speeches,' he says, 'but I do enjoy doing something so different from my day job. And the money's cool.'

Once you have your idea (or ideas) it's time to discuss it/ them with others. The temptation is to ask your friends and family – the people who know you best – for their advice. Or to send some emails to people already in that industry or space. Both of these are bad ideas. Assuming that they're kind and supportive, your friends will tell you whatever you want to hear. And the industry old-timer, scarred by years at the coalface, will usually give you 10 reasons why it won't work.

So instead, ask the smartest people you know or the smartest people you can access. Ask your boss's boss, or your mum's lawyer mate, or your dad's accountant – people who are close enough to listen, but remote (and clever) enough to pick holes. And you do want some holes picking. After all, regardless of the idea, you're going to have to put some money into this thing. You want your maths to be sound and your logic to be watertight. In other words, you want to be challenged a bit. 'You want a polarized reaction,' says LinkedIn co-founder Reid Hoffman. 'What you want is some people going, "You guys are out of your minds", and some people going, "I see it".'

Listen to their challenge, of course; use it to refine and hone your idea. But, crucially, don't let them dissuade you entirely. After all, it's not like you're going all-in on this. You're not betting the farm on day one. And, besides, even really, extremely smart people can be really, extremely wrong. 'There is not the slightest indication that nuclear energy will ever be obtainable,' said Albert Einstein in 1932 (today it provides around 10 per cent of the world's energy). 'The horse is here to stay but the automobile is only a novelty, a fad,' said Henry Ford's bank manager. And so on.

You'll also need to buckle up for some bad advice; or not even bad, just obvious to the point of being asinine: 'You should get Gordon Ramsay to use your knives on TV,' one person told me. 'Oh, what a brilliant idea!' I wanted to say. 'I hadn't thought about that. I'll just sort that out now.'

In my experience, the best way around all this is to take it all quite seriously. I found that the quality of advice usually correlated with the effort I put into the meeting. A chance chat in a pub, or a quick conversation over the phone, rarely garnered much helpful insight. Whereas, when I booked a proper meeting, the advice improved greatly. I learned a lot from these meetings – about foreign exchange, and the practicalities of postage, and the importance of authenticity in branding (I'd always thought it was better to pretend that I was a big, trustworthy company, but early customers often actually prefer that you're small). So seek out clever, intelligent challenge and listen; but never be dissuaded entirely.

GETTING GOING

Having chatted with your smartest pals and honed the idea, your next task is to decide your risk appetite. Do you want to make, buy or hold stock which allows you to offer speedy delivery? Or do you want to sell based on pre-orders? Paynter Jacket Co. – a London-based maker of, yep, jackets – does exactly this. Their limited edition collections are sold in four batches a year, with customers having to wait two months to take delivery after purchasing. Which sounds like a colossal arse ache, but in reality people go mad for the delayed gratification. Not least because it prevents Paynter from wasting any fabric. 'Our jackets have sold out in as little as 86 seconds,' says the Paynter website. 'We'd recommend adding our email address to your . . . contacts to avoid missing out.'

You'll also need to spend some money. It doesn't matter how small or hokey your business is going to be, you're going to need a name, a logo and some other creative assets like product photography. Don't skimp on these. People are willing to spend money with new brands, not crap ones. And while you might be able to call in some favours with a designer friend, my recommendation is to do it properly. You'll just have more input, more control and a greater ability to ask for amends. Websites like Fiverr have radically democratised design and web development meaning that, with just a few clicks, anyone can access brilliant creatives for a few hundred quid. So do that.

Do you really need a website? Yes. Absolutely, unquestionably, irrefutably.

It doesn't matter if you're upcycling furniture, helping someone with their sales strategy or teaching cello, if you're asking
people for money, you need a website.

Thankfully building one yourself – and a really very good
one at that – has never been easier. Even I managed to drag
and drop something half decent, and I'm what you would
call 'utterly pants with tech' (if you were being generous).

The main trade-off between the big website building
services (Wix, Shopify, Squarespace, etc.) is customisation
versus ease of use. Wix, for example, is known for being
almost completely customisable. You can put buttons
wherever you want, add pictures and video, move stuff
around, but, for the uninitiated or impatient, it's also pretty
hard work. Shopify, in contrast, is much easier to set up,
but the design parameters are more rigid. The moment you
want to move this box or add that feature, you have to
cough up for professional help. Squarespace is unquestionably the strongest for blogging or content-driven businesses
(photography, catering, etc.), but it can be quite expensive
and its e-commerce offering isn't as jazzy as Shopify. So
have a good play around with each of them before making
your choice.

Armed with an idea, a logo and a workable website, you
can start selling. Lots of people worry about this, but in my
experience it's the easiest bit. Certainly it's easier than actually making the damned things or even finding a packaging
supplier (that was a fun weekend). There are just so many
different ways to go about acquiring customers, and none of

them require the 'gift of the gab', advertising budgets or glitzy launch parties. In my experience, the most effective marketing methods are usually the free ones. They require thought, time and effort. But other than that, you needn't max out your credit cards.

Take, for example, the food-related newsletter I email out every Friday. At fewer than 500 words it's not exactly *Don Quixote*, but for some reason people enjoy my recipe finds and restaurant recommendations. And even though I've only got 2,000 subscribers, I almost always sell a few knives in the hours after sending it. I'm not alone in this – according to research from marketing firm AWeber, nearly 60 per cent of marketers say that email is an effective or very effective tool for acquiring new customers.

Instagram, too, is huge. I try to do a minimum of three posts a week – some about food, some about knives. And there's definitely a correlation between how a post performs and the number of orders I get. Not always. Sometimes a picture of a new product will be a smash hit on Instagram, but a total flop commercially. Just because someone 'likes' or 'shares' something, doesn't mean they'll buy it. Which is infuriating, but keep on trucking. In my experience, the platform really rewards consistency and quality. And whenever they launch a new feature to the app, be sure to focus your efforts on that. Anecdotal evidence suggests that Instagram incentivises/rewards accounts that support new features by inserting their content into people's 'Explore' feeds. In other words, it pays to swim with Instagram's own corporate objectives.

Then there's the blog. Eurgh, *the blog*. I hate doing the blog. It's one of those annoying things that's both really hard work and really effective, meaning that I can't shirk it. If it didn't work, I wouldn't have to do it. But it does. It always bloody does. So rather than spending my evenings doing what I love (stroking the dog, eating pasta, watching *Grand Designs*), I'm chained to my desk hacking out 500 words on the history of kitchen knives. There are two reasons why the blog works. Firstly, if I write the right things people will share them with their friends who – fingers crossed – might end up buying one of my knives. Secondly (and more importantly), the blog helps me to climb Google's search rankings. Entire books have been written and university courses taught on the vagaries of Google's search algorithm. But one of the few universally accepted truths is that the more brilliant, helpful content you produce, the more Google will send people your way.

As well as the free stuff, I've also occasionally paid for marketing. I've bought adverts on Instagram and Facebook, and done a few bits on Google, too. Each platform has its own (usually pretty intuitive) self-service platform. So with a little bit of reading and clicking about, you can be up and advertising in a few hours. Just be sure to set your daily spending limits or else you'll wake up one morning to discover you've spent £500 on advertising by mistake and have to beg your mother for a loan. *I definitely have not done this.*

The obvious place to start searching for customers is your friendship group. My advice would be not to do this. There are a few reasons why. Firstly, someone being your friend doesn't mean they're your ideal customer. Most of my friends, for example, are rubbish at cooking. And even among those who are into it, I doubt many would be keen on a £100 knife. Focusing my efforts on selling to them would be ineffective for me and irritating for them. Secondly, there's also the fact that, now that everyone has their 'thing', a kind of crowding out takes place. Where once your friends might have leapt to support your entrepreneurialism, now they're likely fatigued. It's the same with charity fun runs and baked bean baths – the first time you get a Virgin Money Giving email you can't wait to cough up your £20 (plus Gift Aid), but by the time the tenth one arrives your generosity is starting to wane.

Finally, even if your friends are into your idea and do support you, that raises a troubling question. Namely, is your business actually any good or do you just have kind and supportive friends? And, more importantly, can you make accurate investment decisions based on your sales numbers? Or are you going to place a monster order for supplies only to discover that you've exhausted your pals and that real people don't want your products after all?

Focusing your efforts on selling to real punters not only swerves all these problems, it also means you'll get much better, more honest feedback. No real friend is going to tell you your packaging sucks or your delivery is too slow. Strangers, in contrast, will give you both barrels and that's to be welcomed. They'll tell you what's great about your product and what's rubbish about your website. They'll reward hard work with five-star reviews and punish laziness with refund requests. Above all, they'll vote with their wallets. If you're doing something brilliant, they'll buy. If you're taking the piss or under-delivering, they'll go elsewhere. That's been my experience.

> While positive feedback feels better, negative opinions are always more helpful.

All this is not to suggest, however, that you shouldn't utilise your friends and network. It's just that their value to you isn't in sales, it's in scaling your marketing. It's in helping you gain access to their own networks – their five-aside team, their work mates, the parents from their kid's school – people who you'd otherwise have to spend hundreds of pounds advertising to. And, crucially, people who – if they do buy from you – buy because they really want to. Better still, unlike you trying to sell them your first batch of brownies, facilitating these introductions costs your friends nothing. They can subscribe to, like and share your social content for free. They can create and post content of their own using your products. They can forward your newsletter to interested parties. They can distribute a 'friends and family' promo code granting their network a discount or deal. They can help you with targeted introductions – to journalist friends or other side hustlers for potential partnerships. And all the while, they'll never have to pay you a penny.

If you get this kind of network marketing right, the results can be utterly bonkers. Pick almost any start-up 'unicorn' from the past 10 years and doubtless network marketing will have been central to their success. Do you remember Uber's referral codes, for example? Or Monzo's 'skip the queue' friend pass which allowed you to open a bank account faster? That one worked so well that, according to Monzo's founder Tom Blomfield, Monzo was able to acquire 60,000 new customers each month with zero marketing spend. Today they're valued at £1.2 billion.

Obviously, most of us side hustlers aren't shooting for that scale, but the point stands – ask your friends for their help, rather than their money. And whatever you do, don't be embarrassed. Never fret about asking your mates for support and never feel queasy about doing something different. This is your side hustle – it's supposed to be different. If you want to be a recruiter by day and a dance instructor by night, then do it. If you want to sell scarves, or build furniture, or print T-shirts, or cook paella at festivals, then why not?

And when the inevitable happens and some know-it-all bore makes a snarky comment about your new venture, you must ignore them. No, better than that, feel sorry for them and their dull, torpid little lives. Because that's what they are, these people – they're boring, bland, insecure, missionary-with-the-lights-off people. And we should call them out.

Of course, ignoring the doubters is easier said than done. The question to ask yourself is, 'Has anyone less qualified than me achieved this? And if so, why can't I?' That might sound a bit cocksure or hubristic, but I promise it isn't. Because once you start interrogating the skills and experience of side hustlers or business owners who you admire, very quickly you realise just how similar they are to you.

They don't have MBAs, or crazy connections, or oodles of money. Most of them are just people with an idea and a work ethic. Like Jack Darley, a wedding photographer who makes and sells chopping boards on the side. Or Jo and Jess, two foodie sisters who run a weekly restaurant pop-up, The Flygerians, selling delicious Nigerian dishes to hungry crowds. Or Elizabeth Macneal, author of several beautiful books, who also has a wonderful ceramics business. Peruse any of these folks' Instagrams or websites and you'd doubtless be intimidated by their professionalism and achievements. At least from the outside, each of them seems streaks ahead. But they're also just people. Jack, Jo, Jess and Elizabeth are just humans hunting for a little extra excitement, a fraction more income. Beyond their passion, intelligence and hard work, their only differentiation is their ideas. You've got an idea. And you're passionate, intelligent and hard-working.

So, assuming you're happy in your primary career, what are you waiting for?

WILL I SURVIVE A SPELL OF UNEMPLOYMENT?

I'VE BEEN FIRED twice.

Surprising, I know. Given my disinterest and career clumsiness, you'd expect it to be a lot more. But somehow my professional life expectancy hasn't been that bad.

The first firing wasn't that awful. I was 18 at the time and working as a waiter at a wedding. The evening started badly and got worse. First the bride's mother busted me eating canapés ('You horrible oik!'). Then, while clearing a half-eaten platter of *fruits de mer*, I managed to biff the icy, fishy water down a bridesmaid's neck. And then, as a final flourish, one of the uncles caught me sharing a ciggie with his daughter. This proved fatal. 'You simply can't deal drugs to the guests,' said Cindy the boss.

'It was only a Marlboro Light,' I protested. 'I wasn't cutting smack.'

'I'm sorry,' said Cindy, while binning some chronically overcooked chicken wrapped in Parma ham (this being 2008), 'you'll have to go.'

The second sacking hurt more. If you can recall my patchwork quilt of a career, this was the job selling Microsoft Excel courses to accountants. It was only ever a filler job (one of the many I took to hit my 'number' while writing my first book), but losing it still hurt. And not just because I really, really needed the money; I'd also gone all-in on it. I'd made the fundamental mistake of thinking I might be good at it and had no other irons in the fire. So, when they sacked me, not only was I broke, I was also starting again from scratch.

This is not to say that my sacking was a surprise. After less than a month I seemed destined for the trash can. There were two key problems. Firstly, and most obviously, I wasn't very good at it. It was mostly a home-working gig and that meant motivation was an issue. Faced with the option of cold-calling *another* regional accountancy firm or learning 'Let It Be' on my keyboard, I almost always opted for the latter. And even on those days when I did summon the fortitude to ring Bore & Snore LLP ('Swansea's leading accountancy est. 1985'), I never once actually sold an Excel training course. I was quite adept at getting them on the phone, and occasionally I talked them into receiving a proposal, but, try as I might, the buggers never bit.

The second problem was the boss. He seemed an odd, unhappy man called Alexander Hamilton. 'Like the guy from the musical?' I asked on day one. 'What's a musical?'

came his reply. I knew then that our time together would be short.

He also had some very wacky ways of working. He thought they were cool and Silicon Valley-y, but to me they just seemed weird. Like the fact that everyone had an inflatable mattress under their bed for midday naps. Or that he kept the office at 15°C to 'aid productivity'. Or that he told me to visit my clients' offices unannounced and wait in the lobby until they gave me a meeting. 'You're joking, surely?' I asked. Reader, he was not.

So I limped along for two months and got sacked the day before my probation ended. The firing itself wasn't at all how I'd imagined it. Having witnessed hundreds of sackings during my consulting stint, I thought I'd be well prepared. I knew that people usually react in one of three ways to being laid off: they're extremely angry, or they're confused, or they're quietly resigned. Of the three, I'd always thought I was the angry type. 'Fuck you!' I thought I'd say. 'You're making a big mistake! You haven't seen the last of me!'

In reality, though, I was the quiet one. My primary emotion wasn't so much furious indignation as, well, sadness. Even if you hate a job or know that you're no good at it, you still want to be the person who quits. You want to jump before being pushed. You want to be the one who books Pizza Express and does the dumping ('it's not you, it's me'), not the saddo dumpee sobbing into a portion of dough balls. Sitting in that freezing cold meeting room, all manner of anxious thoughts whizzed around my head. There was financial panic, obviously. Would I miss the rent? Would I have to cancel our holiday? Could I still afford an engagement ring? But above all, I just felt a deep, hollow sense of uselessness.

In the UK today, around 1 in 20 (around 5 per cent) of us is unemployed. That's a bit better than what had been expected post-pandemic, and it's nowhere near as bad as the eighties when 10 per cent of people were out of work. But it's still crap. Beneath those macro *News at Ten* statistics lie thousands of individual struggles and tragedies. People who want to work – *need* to work – but can't. People whose lack of work forces them to make impossible choices – between feeding themselves or heating their homes, between which child needs new shoes more. People who suffer profound, long-term psychological trauma as a result of being jobless. The statistics and research here are very clear. Unemployed people are not only more likely to struggle with sleep, appetite and lower sex drive, they're also much more prone to anxiety and depression.

My own experience – thank goodness – wasn't as bad as all that. Not because of my brilliance, but thanks to pure luck. As serendipity had it, after two months of scrabbling around, an old colleague called me with a contract gig which I grasped with both hands. Mind you, it was still a rough couple of months. My overriding memory is one of terrific boredom. There's no escaping how dull applying for jobs and waiting to hear back is. It's hours and hours spent clicking and typing, rejigging your CV, trying to fill a side of A4 for a covering letter. In many cases it's harder work than most work.

Plus, you can't do anything fun when you're unemployed. You can't afford to. Or even if you can afford it, the guilt of spending what little money you have far outweighs the pleasure it delivers. Of course, there are plenty of free things you can do (and, boy, do the employed love reminding you of this). You can walk in a park, for example. Or sit in a park. Or lie in a park. Or jog in a park. Or something else . . . in a park. Or if parks aren't your thing, you can always visit a museum.

Beyond the boredom come the flashes of panic – little moments in which you realise how utterly buggered you are, how stupid you've been and how desperate your future is. It's like being trapped in one of those awful anxiety dreams where you've cheated on your partner, or stolen something, or murdered someone. As though you've done something horrific and there's no going back.

There was also embarrassment; shame at being nearly 30 years old and unable to support myself. At my age, my parents had already moved out of London and had my oldest brother. My dad was quietly, determinedly climbing the corporate ladder and providing for his new family. Meanwhile, here I was, some useless, privileged toad who, despite years of fancy schooling and covetous career opportunities, couldn't cobble together the rent.

And it wasn't just my parents who I looked to for benchmarking. My mates, too, were a healthy source of comparison. At the exact moment when I was a penniless, unemployed schlub, they were all getting promotions and bigger flats and posher cars. Or that's how it seemed to me. All of which fed this bizarre, poisonous paranoia that I was going to be left behind. They'd all keep on keeping on, and pretty soon I'd be the broke ex-mate who couldn't keep up. No more dinner invites, birthday parties or weekends away for me. 'Do we have to invite Josh?' they'd say on their secret WhatsApp group. 'Dinner will be £50 a head and it's just awkward.' Privileged, melodramatic and very 'millennial', I know. But it's also how I felt.

I worried intensely that this was it, that I'd be unemployed forever. Or if not unemployed forever, that I couldn't get the kinds of jobs I once could. It felt like I'd been booted out of a club and wouldn't be readmitted. One of the many platitudes we get fed about career moves is that, if it all goes pear-shaped, we can always go back to our old job. And intuitively this makes sense. After all, it's not like your skills, network or insight wither overnight. You'll still remember all the lingo and have all the same contacts. Why wouldn't your former employer (or a similar one) welcome you back with open arms? No?

Well, logically, yes. Except when you've made a move and it hasn't paid off, you don't really care about logic. Whiling away the hours of unemployment you start to wonder whether your decision to try something new has blotted your copybook. Even though I'd left advertising sales without burning bridges, I'd still made the decision to leave. I'd still chosen to move on, to try something new. Even the most level-headed, generous boss would surely see that as a red flag? Just as a marriage is never the same after an affair, so, too, was my CV now tinged with professional infidelity. And, besides, all of that's assuming that the old job hasn't already been snapped up by some young, gun-slinging whipper snapper.

Obviously, as it happened, none of that turned out to be true. The chap who hired me out of unemployment didn't care at all that I'd spent some time out of work. My careerist friends haven't abandoned me (yet). And as far as I can tell, my parents still love me. But at the time it all felt very real. Very real, very scary and very depressing.

UNEMPLOYMENT: A USER'S GUIDE

Under normal circumstances, I'm not usually a 'user's guide' or manual kinda guy. Like most (unjustifiably) overconfident men, my usual preference is instead to 'learn by doing'. Whether it's changing tyres or installing software, I'd sooner tear out my own eyeballs than read the guide explaining how to do it properly. Better to just get going, no matter how inefficient or ineffective it might be.

What's weird is that I know how illogical and infuriating this 'philosophy' is, and yet I seem incapable of change. Our flat is strewn with half-built Ikea furniture and Wi-Fi enabled printers that are neither connected to the Wi-Fi, nor capable of printing; and yet, still, I steadfastly continue to half-arse things.

That said, there is one area of life, one user's manual, which I would have read voraciously – the guide to navigating unemployment. Being jobless is just such a confusing, intimidating, austere time that even I would have seen fit to break my golden rule. And I'm willing to bet it'll be the same for you. So here's my brief guide for moving through unemployment – I hope you find it helpful.

I. DON'T PANIC

People behave weirdly when they panic. They think weird things, they do weird things, they make choices which defy logic and act in ways which run counter to their own self-interest. Stress not only induces a physiological response (raised heart rate and blood pressure, the release of adrenaline and cortisol), it also stimulates a psychological one, too. We're less rational when we're stressed, as well as being more impulsive and open to risk-taking.

The reason for this, according to a study by researchers at the Massachusetts Institute of Technology (MIT), is that stress shifts the dynamics within a specific brain circuit which starts in the medial prefrontal cortex (responsible for mood) and extends to a cluster of neurons called striosomes (responsible for habit formation, motivation and reward). It's in this part of the brain where we balance the pros and cons of different options and decide on courses of action. Unless, of course, we're stressed. If that happens, the function of this circuit is impaired, causing us to drastically underestimate risks and overestimate rewards. Which, in turn, becomes a vicious circle – we're impulsive because we're stressed and that impulsivity only makes us more stressed.

Recognising this, acknowledging that when we're stressed we make crap decisions, informs the first (and most important) rule of Unemployment Club: remain calm. Because while everyone's path to joblessness is different, the temptation to panic is ubiquitous and always unhelpful. Whether you're freshly unemployed, momentarily 'in between gigs' or have been drifting for months, the danger is that you slump into irrationality and panic your way into poor decisions. That might mean taking a job you know you'll hate or applying for jobs you know you're not right for. Either way, every moment spent stressed and illogical is a moment not spent on the important work of uncovering your future.

That sounds dramatic, but it's true. Everyone I've spoken to who's been unemployed recalls applying for or even taking a job out of panic. I was no different. Even today my desktop remains littered with the PDFs of panicked job applications past. 'Josh CV: Events Coordinator' or 'Covering Letter: PR Officer'. All of which was a terrific waste of time, while also being terrible for the psyche. Because, to be clear, I was never going to be a PR Officer. I knew that and – after even a cursory glance at my totally irrelevant CV – the employer would know it, too. But still I applied. Still I took half a day to research the role, tweak my CV and write a covering letter because, well, why not? It was something to do, something to make me feel purposeful, something I could say to Cali when she came home.

In reality, though, all I was doing was setting myself up for an inevitable fall when, two weeks later, I'd get the rejection email. 'Unfortunately your application for Head of the World Bank is no longer under consideration.' And, again, it's a vicious cycle. The more you panic, the more you apply for inappropriate jobs, the more you get rejected, the more you panic, the more outrageous your applications become, and so on.

Psychologists call this urge to do something (anything!) our 'bias to action'. And in some circumstances it's considered a good thing. In a fast-paced industry, like technology for example, it's usually better to do something, make mistakes and iterate than to sit around waiting for a perfect solution while your competitors pull ahead. Why else would Amazon include 'bias for action' as one its 16 'Leadership Principles'?

But business aside, there are lots of areas of life where bias to action is bad. It's what makes investors fiddle with their portfolios when they'd be better off doing nothing. It's what makes doctors run tests on patients with non-urgent symptoms, when it would be less costly (and often quicker) to simply wait and see. It's what makes football goalkeepers dive to the left or right during penalty shootouts rather than following the optimal strategy of staying in the middle. And, most importantly for us, it's what causes unemployed people to panic and make bad decisions.

My argument here isn't that we should do nothing; it's that we should apply rationality before doing anything. Don't rush into applications that you won't get. Don't waste time rewriting your CV for companies you have no intention of working for. Don't flail and flap. Instead, breathe. Take your time. Think. Use the first few days of your unemployment to uncover (or rediscover) your professional purpose, plot your plans A to Z and then get cracking. 'No need to panic,' you can say to yourself. 'I've got a strategy and I'm sticking to it.'

> Having a proper, rational plan not only increases the likelihood of success, it also reduces associated anxiety.

The biggest cause of unemployment panic (and ergo the biggest driver of bad decision-making) is money. Joblessness makes even the most profligate panic about their income and outgoings. With the taps turned off and the plughole open, your cash and savings drain away at an alarming rate, and the temptation to take the first job you're offered can be overwhelming.

Resist this if you can. Instead, use the time to reflect and reaffirm what you want from your career and chart a course towards achieving it. And if you need a 'money job' to make ends meet then fine; just be crystal clear about what that job is and what it is not. It's an interim gig, a means to an end, a way of keeping the wolf from the door, but one which also allows you to uncover and move towards your 'forever job'. You might consider it embarrassing to go from your old gig to cleaning tables or answering phones, but wouldn't it be more embarrassing (let alone depressing) to spend your whole life ricocheting from one misfitting job to another without ever finding a rhythm or direction?

2. WORK SMART

The second, cast-iron rule of being unemployed is to work smart. And when I say 'cast-iron rule' what I really mean is 'thing I wish I'd done'. I worked hard when I was unemployed. I set myself daily targets for applications. I wrote and rewrote my CV many, many times. I spent entire days crafting covering letters to companies I'd never hear back from. And I did all of this, five days a week, 10 hours a day for two months.

I shouldn't have. Not only because it was a fantastically dull, depressing way to spend my life, but, more importantly, because it didn't work. Grafting away, manically scouring LinkedIn and drilling out applications didn't move me anywhere closer to a great job. It got me almost no interviews, and not a single job offer. Even roles much more junior than those I'd been doing, sailed by without so much as a 'Thanks for your application' email.

My mistake was equating effort with outcome. I thought the more I did, the shorter my unemployment would be. Which makes sense. In most areas of life, the harder you work, the quicker and better the outcome. The faster you can break eggs, the sooner you'll have a lovely omelette. The harder you practise your golf swing, the better your game gets. And so on.

But in job-hunting the opposite is true. Because at any one time, the number of roles you should apply for will be pretty small. Think about it. Your ideal job will be one that's (a) available; (b) desirable; and (c) attainable. And (unless you set your sights very broadly) there just won't be that many of those kicking around. Five maybe? Seven at a push. And say one or two new ones become available each week. That's a maximum of 36 jobs a month worth applying for. Which, divided by the number of working days in the month, makes 1.8 applications a day. In other words, if you're doing more than two applications a day, you're likely wasting time.

I'm not suggesting you become a layabout. Far from it. The nano successes I mentioned earlier – getting up early, making your bed, doing laundry – take on an even greater significance when you're unemployed. Unemployment is a time when self-esteem is in short supply and when simple things like exercising, shaving and getting dressed can be the difference between self-worth and self-hatred. So do all that; just don't focus so much on applications. Do fewer of them and spend more time on the stuff that will improve your applications and interviews. Read around the role, research it, study the company and its competitors, download its annual reports, watch those videos of the CEO at a conference. And think. Think about why you're perfect for that job. Think about why that job is perfect for you. Think about how you fit with the company and how you're going to help it grow.

Because job-hunting is competitive. It's perhaps the most intense, impactful sport on earth. It might not feel like that when you're scrolling job adverts while watching *This Morning* ('coming up after the break we meet a woman who says she's in love with the ghost of her husband's brother'), but in my experience it's a war zone. Just look at the numbers. According to jobsite Glassdoor, the average corporate job advert receives over 250 applications. And post-pandemic, there are signs that those numbers have grown exponentially. During the peak of the first lockdown in March 2020, jobs which used to receive about 30 applications were seeing hundreds, while the most popular roles were getting thousands of applicants. A role as an entry-level paralegal, for example, drew a whopping 4,228 applications. Naturally (and thankfully) those numbers won't stay that way forever. But the simple fact is that we're not alone in wanting what we want. And, while getting your application in early has to be a good thing, it's far better to make it brilliant; far better to be the person whose CV fits perfectly, whose covering letter oozes insight and thought.

3. MAKE IT QUICK

The greatest psychological trauma of unemployment isn't the anger at being let go, or the uselessness, or even the boredom and money worries, it's the sense that the longer you go without work, the less likely you are to get work. It's feeling that your CV is somehow infected, riddled with a career cancer which is growing bigger and more malignant each day. Until, presumably, you reach a point where it's terminal – where you're no longer just unemployed, but also unemployable.

I spent ages thinking and panicking about this. And while I'd love to tell you that it isn't a thing – that finding employment doesn't get harder the longer you're unemployed – I'm afraid that would be a lie. The data here is very robust: the more protracted our unemployment, the less likely we are to find work. In fact, this phenomenon is so entrenched that labour economists have given it its own name: 'negative duration dependence'. And while it affects all of us, some folks are particularly prone to it. The older we are, for example, the longer our unemployment is likely to be.

How very depressing, I know. And it would be, except for the fact that two of the biggest determinants of 'negative duration dependence' are things that we can control. It's not that employers stop wanting us, or that our personal networks disintegrate, or that our skills wither. Instead, the two biggest factors are deteriorating search effort over time (pretty obviously you try harder in Week 1 than Week 20) and a curious mismatch between our expectations and the realities of job-hunting (people who are long-term unemployed tend to overestimate their ability to find a job and as a result don't apply for jobs they can get, or hold out for something better).

I'm not suggesting that these factors are easy to overcome, but they are at least overcomeable. And, given the choice, I'd always prefer my future to be determined by me and my actions rather than by factors or fate outside of my command. Not because I'm brilliant, but because at least then there are no excuses. There can be no passing the buck, no wailing at the wind, if things don't go the way I want.

Of the two, I think that maintaining search effort is the easier. Focus and dogged determination are not traits which I possess in abundance, but even I can get into the swing of a daily routine. Which is what this is all about. Research shows that with regular repetition it's possible to automate behaviour in as little as 18 days. It doesn't matter if you're learning the piano or going teetotal, if you can exhibit the same behaviour for three weeks you've got a good shot of habitualising it. So get up at the same time every day, exercise, plan your mornings and afternoons, and, importantly, plan to waste time. Yes, *plan to waste time.* As humans, we have a natural propensity (and I'd argue an inalienable right) to procrastinate. Wasting a few hours making lunch or stalking an ex on Instagram is all part of the normal human experience. You'd do it if you had a job, and you'll do it when you don't. And, as long as you're not doing it to the detriment of your job search, the only problem with wasting time is if it makes you panic or feel sad: 'Bugger, I've spent a whole morning watching cat videos. Why am I so useless?' Being deliberate about it allows us to avoid all that negativity: 'It's now time to spend 15 minutes on Asos.' Procrastinating becomes part of the plan; something you need to do, not something to panic about.

In a similar vein, it's really important to know when your day is done and to recognise when your productivity has dipped below the point of usefulness; again, quality over quantity. As above, we want to be working smart, not hard.

Set yourself targets and goals for each day, and stop when you've achieved them.

Again, the research here is clear. Applying for roles isn't just the worst part of being unemployed, it also becomes more painful the longer you're doing it – in Week 1 you're excited to get going; by Week 10 you'd sooner take a cheese knife to your own genitals than write another covering letter. Feeling like this is normal and having a clear, habitual daily routine will help ameliorate it. But more than anything, unemployment demands that we treat ourselves with exponential kindness. The longer we're unemployed, the more generous and sympathetic we must become. This isn't an argument for laziness or low effort, but if you've hit your daily goals and want to go for a walk, then do. If you've finished the day's research and a friend invites you to the pub, then go. Try to embrace and enjoy the little upsides of unemployment – the flexibility, the autonomy, the daytime TV.

The second determinant of 'negative duration dependency' is this business of knowing when to take a job and when to hold out for something better and is altogether more tricky. Throughout our lives we're taught that ambition and backing oneself are good things. And they are. They have to be, don't they? Achieving greatness, being the best, feeling fulfilled – aren't these things that we should all want for ourselves?

Well, maybe. Except there is also definitely an inflexion point where backing ourselves becomes a problem, where ambition becomes hubris and where our pride becomes self-defeating. I'm not advocating for mediocrity or 'settling', but we do have to be realistic. If the economy is tanking, or your dream industry is in turmoil, or you're pivoting into a new field, you might have to take a short-term hit for long-term gain. You might have to go back-wards to go forward. As long as there is a clear path to moving forward, that's fine.

I'm not telling you to compromise on your 'why', but accept that you might need a circuitous route to get there. You will get there, though. I promise you that. It might not feel like that as you haul yourself onto Indeed.com on yet another grey, cold Tuesday morning in March, but you will. You'll keep pushing and pushing, working smart and staying alive to opportunity; and pretty soon – almost certainly sooner than you think – you'll get the news you want.

4. KEEP YOUR CHIN UP

Along with 'exams aren't everything' and 'plenty more fish in the sea', the banality I've been told more than any other is 'do try to stay positive'. I'm not sure why, but when you have a mental health problem (and particularly if you're chatty about having one), people tell you to stay positive with near-constant, metronomic regularity. As though the only reason you're struggling with depression or anxiety is because you haven't considered *not* struggling with depression or anxiety. It must – they assume – have slipped your notice that you could just be cheerful instead. You could just put on a happy face and move on, keep smiling, stay laughing, stay positive.

The reason I say all this is because, at first glance, the advice I'm about to give you – to keep your chin up – feels quite obvious and platitudinal. If not a direct sibling of 'stay positive', 'chin up' must at least be a close cousin or aunt. The problem, though, is that it's also essential. In fact, keeping your chin up, maintaining positivity and recognising that losing your job means nothing about you as a person, is the single most important thing about being unemployed. It says nothing about the things that really matter – your generosity, your kindness, your work ethic. It just means you were in the wrong place at the wrong time; or, like me, you weren't very good at it.

'But what will other people think?' Honestly, they won't. I promise. One of the biggest realisations of the past few years is that people really don't care as much as you think they do. They don't notice your hair loss, or spot your weight gain, or ponder your career. They care about you, sure. They're not arseholes. They want to know you're cheery, and purposeful, and – in my case at least – not on the precipice of another breakdown. But beyond that . . . meh. My friends couldn't give a fig if I work as a plumber, or date a porn star, or hawk kitchen knives on Instagram. They're all (rightly) far too busy with their own frenetic, worrisome lives. They haven't got the bandwidth. As long as I'm not in prison, not suicidal and definitely coming for dinner next Friday ('you're on pud'), then that's enough.

Realising all this is a slow, gradual and partial process. And definitely not one that I have completed. The old cliché is that, where in your twenties you care intensely what others think, by the time you reach your thirties you care a little bit less, and so on. The burden of expectation is magically lifted and you begin to waft through life in a warm, happy glow. This has not been my experience. I haven't reached a zen mastery of insecurity. I'm still desperately self-conscious. It's just that the things I'm self-conscious about have changed. It's less about external stuff (my job, my appearance, my clothes) and more internal (how generous people think I am, how interesting they think I am, how funny they think I am), which in a way is deeper and harder to navigate. But it does at least free me from thinking that just because I'm pants at selling Excel courses, I'm a bad or unworthy person.

And I should say, indifference to unemployment isn't limited to our social lives. Employers, too, don't really care.

> Every single boss, manager, hirer and recruiter I've spoken to has said that, as long as you use your time unemployed well, they're open to hiring unemployed people.

They'll ask you about why you left your last job, of course. And you'd better have a convincing argument with plenty of supporting evidence. But beyond that, a spell of jobless-ness isn't a big deal. Primarily because, when you think about it, there are lots of reasons why hiring someone out of unemployment is actually a better option. Not only can unemployed candidates interview and start quicker, but they also usually cost companies less. Partly because (initially at least) companies can drive a harder wage bargain, but also because there are likely to be lower recruitment fees (which typically cost employers 15–20 per cent of the new joiner's annual salary).

'I'm really not bothered by it [unemployment],' Simon Longbottom (CEO of Stonegate Pubs) told me. 'I want to see that you've been constructive, perhaps used the time to retrain or help others. But otherwise we're blind to it. Why wouldn't we be?'

Naturally, not every manager or recruiter will be as progressive. There are bound to be some knuckle-draggers who still see unemployment as a black mark. But do you really want to work for them? Rarely do people with such antiquated views turn out to be motivational or inspiring leaders. Brilliant managers, of the sort you want to work for and grow with, look beyond things like unemployment. Only the second-tier, low-grade folks (who we should avoid at all costs) care about the quotidian. We want to work for Sandberg, Musk or Branson, not David Brent.

And in any case, the world is changing. Soon businesses won't have a choice but to hire people from unemployment because, sadly, it's going to start happening to more and more of us. The dual forces of artificial intelligence (AI) and automation are already upturning industries and displacing hundreds of thousands of jobs. A recent PwC study found that nearly 30 per cent of jobs could be vulnerable by the mid-2030s. And they aren't the jobs you might think. Yes, manual work like bus driving and box packing are particularly at risk. But so, too, are roles in financial services where algorithms are supplanting humans. Or in medicine where surgeries are increasingly performed by robots. Or aviation where trials of unmanned passenger aircraft are advancing at pace. Put simply, where once spells on the dole and career pivots were considered odd or troubling, pretty soon they're going to be the norm. Which won't make them less painful – losing your job hurts regardless of the cause. But it will at least lessen any remaining stigma, and haul those knuckle-draggers into the future.

So keep your chin up. Recognise that being unemployed means nothing about you as a person. Remember that no one who matters (including your friends, family and future employers) will think any less of you for having had a spell out of work. And really, really try to stay smiling. If you must, I'll even permit you to indulge in a little inspiration porn. Some of the most famous, glimmeringly successful people on earth have at some point been unemployed. Before he founded Twitter, Jack Dorsey couldn't get a job in his local shoe shop. Harrison Ford was unemployed for so long that he retrained as a carpenter. Even Oprah – yes, Oprah – did time on the dole after being fired from a job reading the news. So if you need to, you can remember them. Sitting in your pants, as I did, suffering through yet another rejection email, you can close your eyes and imagine a time in the near future when you're IPOing your social network, or starring as Hans Solo, or repeatedly shouting 'You get a car!' to an audience of suburban soccer moms. Or you can just remember that you, your career and your life are enough. Whatever works for you.

HOW CAN I ACTUALLY GET THE JOB?

I KNOW THAT in business, military analogies are a bit eighties, but when I mentioned earlier that the job market is a war zone, I wasn't lying. It doesn't matter if you're unemployed, working full time or drifting listlessly through career creek, with limited roles and thousands of willing, available applicants, the process of applying, interviewing and getting your ideal job can be a fierce, uphill battle.

The stark mathematical realities also mean that companies can be both very picky and, often, extremely rude. In my experience, it's possible to apply for upwards of 50 jobs without ever hearing a peep back from employers. Either they dismiss you without any feedback or you get some generic rubbish; or, worst of all, they don't bother to reply at all. All of which is exhausting, infuriating and deflating, as well as being bizarre – if companies aren't interested in speaking to candidates, why do they bother writing job ads and investing in those tortuous online portals?

Given how painful the process can feel, our aim has to be to make it as short as possible. Take as long as you need to uncover what roles and industries you're after, but then make it snappy. Thankfully, from my conversations with bosses, HR folks and recruiters, it seems there's plenty we can do to make this happen. Some of it is very straightforward (but I'd be surprised if you're doing/have done it all – I certainly didn't). And some of it is less obvious/borderline sneaky. All of it, though, is worth taking note of.

I. DRESS FOR BATTLE

The first crucial step is to look the part. And I'm not talking here about your clothes, grooming or skincare regimen (although, depressingly, attractiveness and career prospects have been shown to be tightly correlated). Instead, it's your digital self which is in desperate need of a makeover.

Over 90 per cent of employers now vet candidates' social media in the first phase of a job application. And while until recently best practice involved locking down (if not deleting) your Instagram and Facebook profiles, nowadays that's not quite right. Because while restricting or shutting down your public profile might prevent something bad coming from your social media, it also prevents anything good happening, too. The aim when job hunting – particularly in an ultra-competitive environment – is to present employers with a single, coherent, easy-to-remember narrative around you as a candidate. And while it's not without its pitfalls, social media can play a central role in telling that story.

So instead of deleting your social media, make it a useful proof point for what you say elsewhere. Give it a good tidy, too. Make sure there's no offensive language (70 per cent of those who get canned at the social media snooping phase fall foul of this) or references to drug- or booze-addled weekends. But otherwise use your social media to lay a trail of deliberate, curated breadcrumbs which recruiters can gobble up to your advantage. If you claim in your covering letter to be interested in specific technology, why not retweet some relevant papers or blog posts? If your CV makes a big deal of your proactivity, how about posting a picture of you at an industry conference? And so on.

Unquestionably the most important thing to get right is your LinkedIn profile. With over 740 million members in more than 200 countries, LinkedIn is the centre of the job-hunting universe. It's where topics and industries are discussed, it's where jobs are posted and it's where bosses and recruiters do their due diligence. At a minimum you need an accurate, up-to-date profile which aligns perfectly with your CV. But if you can, go beyond that and actively engage with the platform. Posting blogs, asking questions and commenting on other people's posts doesn't just show employers that you're active within the industry, it also helps you to climb Google's search rankings, making it easier for recruiters to find you. You might worry that it'll appear disingenuous or opportunistic to only start posting once you're job-seeking, but as long as you're making interesting, thoughtful points and providing content that is of value to the reader, no one will notice, let alone care.

It's also worth exploring the idea of a personal website. It needn't be anything too complex – a simple Wix or Squarespace site will suffice. But it's a place where you can house your CV, links to any relevant work, any blogs you write and your contact details. Remember: the aim here is to create and present a consistent narrative about your skills and experience. Building your own site – albeit a really basic one – helps to reinforce this. It might seem egomaniacal or overly self-promotional, but try not to be squeamish. Folks in the creative industries have been building personal sites for yonks. Just as long as it matches with what you say elsewhere and isn't too over the top, you've got nothing to lose by seizing the initiative and setting the agenda around your employability.

Once you're digitally dressed for battle, the next step is to polish your offline assets. Obviously these should cohere exactly to what you're saying online, and do be honest. Contemplating the ferocity of your competition, you might be tempted to upgrade your qualifications or promote yourself from 'Marketing Trainee' to 'Marketing Manager'. Don't do this. I did it once and it was a terrible idea. Not because I got busted (I didn't), but because I wasted so much time and energy worrying that I might. Sitting in the lobby waiting to be called for my last-round interview I wanted a clear, focused head. Instead, I was riddled with anxiety that I was about to get found out. You'll be the same. And besides, the thrill of getting through to a final round will be nothing compared to the pain of getting rejected because of a fib – so don't bother.

Instead, be honest and authentic, while also having an eye for the CV-sifting software which most medium- to large-sized employers now use. Applicant Tracking Systems (ATSs) are databases which collect, sort and rank candidates' applications based on filters set by the employer. Naturally, HR departments love them because they remove so much of the recruitment legwork (hence why 99 per cent of Fortune 500 companies use them). But, for candidates, they present something of a minefield. Even mistakes as simple as submitting your CV in the wrong file format or using different subject headings – 'Certifications' instead of 'Qualifications', for example – can cost you your application. Indeed, according to hiring expert Brie Reynolds, as many as 70 per cent of CVs submitted to ATSs get rejected because they don't meet the system's formatting requirements or desired qualifications.

That said, it's also perfectly possible to turn the ATS to your advantage with some basic tactics. It's always better, for example, to fill in the employer's hiring portal, rather than to follow the 'upload your CV' route. And if there's no option to do this manually, do your best to make your documents ATS-friendly. Use fonts which are ubiquitous (Arial, Helvetica); avoid having any tables or funky formatting; and save the document as a simple PDF. Content-wise, best practice is to list your experience chronologically and to include relevant keywords wherever possible. If the job description calls for 'data analysis skills, including monthly reporting on key KPIs' then – guess what – somewhere in your CV you're going to mention your data analysis skills including your monthly reporting experience. You don't have to parrot the job description word for word, but the main thrust of each requirement should be referenced in your CV.

Doing all of this takes time, energy and determination. But you've got all those things in abundance. And, what's more, because we're eschewing the 'apply for as many jobs as possible' ideology in favour of fewer, better, more targeted applications, it shouldn't be too burdensome. Some of it can even be templated. After all, if you did the thinking and planning correctly, you'll be applying for gigs that are broadly similar. You might need a couple of different CVs (say a sales role CV and a sales and marketing one), but if you're writing wildly different versions that's a sign that you still don't know what you want.

2. KNOW YOUR ENEMY

On average, hiring managers and recruiters spend between six and eight seconds looking at a CV before deciding to reject or proceed with a candidate. Not minutes, seconds. Your fate is sealed in the same time it takes a bee to flap its wings 1,200 times, or for Eminem to rap 40 words, or for Bill Gates to make $1,300 (I know, depressing).

First impressions, therefore, aren't important – they're everything. Job applications have to grab readers in an instant and compel them to put you in the 'to interview' pile. There are a few ways to achieve this effect, but the most powerful and ubiquitous seem to be research and personalisation. Every employer I've spoken to – from pub owners and security bosses, to Big Four accountants – has mentioned the power of a personalised, deeply researched and intelligent application. They want to see that you've taken the time to know their company, to understand how they make money, who their competitors are, who their leaders are and what they think about key industry issues. And they want to see all of this early in the application – right at the start of your covering letter or in the introductory blurb at the top of your CV. Don't be proud here.

Hi Maria,

Apologies for the cold note, but I wanted to get in touch having just watched your speech at Industry Con 2.0. It was so refreshing to hear a different point of view on [industry issue] and, as a long-term admirer of [company], I'd love to discuss any potential roles you have in [department].

For context, I'm 27 years old and have been working in [industry] for the past [X] years (most recently at [employer]). I'm now looking to join a dynamic, fast-growing business focused on [something]. Which is why, naturally, I'm so drawn to [company].

I've attached my CV here.

Would a brief coffee/call be of interest?

Best,

Josh

Remember, you've only got six seconds, so be as flirty and direct as you feel necessary.

And, importantly, maintain your research effort throughout the application and interview process. Nowadays, interviewers don't care if you've got tattoos or if you forget to write a thank you note. But they do want you to have thought about the role, the company and the industry; and to have smart, succinct questions. So spend plenty of time ahead of the meeting noting thoughtful, relevant questions and, if you can, do some social media snooping of your own. I'm convinced that's how I got the job at the bank. The guy hiring me didn't have a Facebook of his own. But through some Internet-based skulduggery, I found his son's account and from there it became obvious that he and his dad were nuts about skiing. Within a few minutes I jotted 'I'm a novice, but very enthusiastic skier' into the hobbies section of my CV. And when they asked me for an interview I spent hours researching snow conditions and watching pro skiing videos. A little creepy perhaps, but when it comes to job interviews, creepiness pays. Within five minutes of the interview starting he'd taken the bait and the rest of it went like a dream. The best interviews are two-way conversations and if a small quantity of social media sneakiness can grease those conversational wheels, then we'd be mad not to do it.

3. STRIKE FIRST

So far we've assumed that the job you're applying for already exists. It's there, advertised on the company's website, just waiting for your brilliantly researched, personalised, ATS-friendly application (which is supported by an engaging and thoughtful social media presence).

Lots of people find jobs they love by following this passive process. But the reality of today's job market is such that, if you can, it's usually better to apply proactively. Not only because it can enable you to nab the gig before others have the chance to, but also because it's easier to demonstrate your research, personalisation and intelligence in a proactive approach. Research from LinkedIn suggests that a whopping 85 per cent of all jobs are filled before they make it to job sites. That means that, for every three roles that make it online, there were another 17 that didn't. Your chances of success are just far, far higher when you go proactive.

Nowadays, it's also often easier to go direct. Fiddling around with online portals can be desperately time-consuming and frustrating, particularly when you have no idea if it's actually reaching the right people. By being proactive, however, you can swerve all that. So what if they don't reply to your email or LinkedIn message? At least you know they've had a chance to see it.

The question is how to go about embarking on a proactive approach. And the answer – as so often with jobs – is research and networking.

The research bit is partly what we just spoke about: understanding the company, its objectives and its competitors. But also it's about the individuals within the business who are going to be crucial to your hiring. At a minimum you want to try to identify three people within each firm: a potential colleague, your potential boss and your potential boss's boss. The plan is to work out who these people are, what challenges they're facing and how you can help out. Traditional sales theory dictates that in any pitch process you're likely to encounter four types of people: budget holders (the people who will be paying for you); champions (someone who's already sold on hiring you); influencers (folks who could be swayed either way); and blockers (people who can kill the deal). Mapping out who's who will enable you to further tailor and personalise your approach. In particular, you want to sniff out a champion and identify the blockers. They're the people with the most potential to make or break your hiring, so it's crucial to begin cultivating relationships with them.

LinkedIn and Google are obviously your best friends here, but you can also do some old-school, face-to-face work, too. One trick I've heard repeatedly is to try to meet with someone who does the job you'd like, but in a different industry. And someone who does a different job, but in the right industry. Splicing together the feedback from these two conversations should help you to really understand where your dream role fits into your ideal industry. And, as long as you ask politely, my experience is that folks are usually up for it. After all, who doesn't enjoy droning on about how important and impactful their job is?

Once you've done all that, you can make the approach. There are lots of different ways to do this, but, from my chats, email is still the best. First you have to guess the individuals' email addresses, which is easy enough. The three most common email formats are: joe@company.com (most used by small companies), jbloggs@company.com (medium-sized ones) and joe.bloggs@company.com (big ones). Send the first email to all three of someone's potential addresses and then note down which two bounce back. And, in the unlikely event that none of them work, you can usually find the company's Communications/PR person's address by reading the 'News' or blog section of their website and adapt this for the person you want to contact. My advice would be to send each of your three prospects a series of three emails, starting with the most senior person and working down.

EMAIL 1

The first email is a version of what hiring experts call a 'pain letter'. It will open with a concise, attention-grabbing nod to your research, before mentioning a problem you imagine they're facing and how you can help. Then it'll close with a neat call to action, but it's pretty hands-off and light-touch. The real purpose of the first email is not to elicit a response, it's to give you an excuse to send a follow-up. On average, email campaigns that include at least one follow-up garner 22 per cent more conversions than those that don't.

Hi Stephanie,

Apologies for the cold note, but having watched your recent speech at Conference 2.0, I wanted to get in touch regarding roles at Epic Corps.

You mentioned in your speech that a key challenge at the moment is finding great software engineers, and as someone with 5+ years' experience in this area (most recently at Competitor Corps), I thought it would be great to connect.

I appreciate that you might not be actively recruiting at the moment, but it would be fantastic if you have a spare 15 minutes for a quick coffee.

I've attached my CV here.

What are your thoughts?

Best,

Josh

EMAIL 2

The second email is pure follow-up and, in my experience, is where you're most likely to get your 'yay' or 'nay'. It should be short and simple, and, most importantly, make it easy for the person to say yes. Nothing is more irritating than an email prod which forces you to go back through your inbox, so be sure to reiterate all the key information.

Often, the trickiest thing is knowing when to send the follow-up. According to the stats, it should be sooner than you might think. Nowadays, the lifespan of an average email is vanishingly short. Indeed, by studying more than 16 billion emails, researchers from the USC Viterbi School of

Engineering found that if someone hasn't replied within 48 hours, the chances of them doing so are almost non-existent. So after two days, it's time for a nudge:

> Hi Stephanie,
>
> Just following up on this – do you have a spare 15 minutes to see if I might help with your engineering challenge? As a reminder, I'm a software engineer with 5+ years of experience (most recently at Competitor Corps). I've reattached my CV here.
>
> Would a coffee/call work in w/c 10th June?
>
> Best,
>
> Josh

EMAIL 3

The third and final email is something of a Hail Mary, but you lose very little by sending it. By this point, assuming they're not dead or on holiday, they've seen one of your emails, and their decision not to reply reflects one of two realities: either they're not interested in hiring you or they are interested but they're too busy. Regardless, there's definitely still value in a final note which makes it even easier for them to say yes.

> Hi Stephanie,
>
> I appreciate you must be extremely busy, so would it make sense for me to connect with someone else in your team initially?
>
> Who would you recommend?
>
> Best,
>
> Josh

Give it another couple of days and, if you still haven't heard back, take their silence as permission to move on to the next person. Of course, you could contact multiple people concurrently, but does the slender time-saving really justify the risk of pissing someone off? And what will you do if they both reply with different answers? We're trying to project an image of ourselves as calm, considered and intelligent, which is antithetical to the whole 'spray and pray' ethos.

The big question, naturally, is: 'Will anyone reply?' And the answer, thankfully, is yes. If you take your time, do the research, write concise and personalised emails and be sure to follow up, at some point someone will reply. It might not be the reply you want, but they will at least reply. And if it is a 'no', then that's fine. At least you know that they have a hiring freeze, or have an internal candidate lined up, or are closing that department. Now you can move on to the next company and narrow your search.

A quick 'no' is always, always better than a drawn-out 'maybe'.

The important thing is to hold your nerve. As we've seen, people do weird things when they're panicked, things which do more harm than good. Resist, for example, the temptation to start cold-calling (badgering folks on the phone is both desperate and irritating). And whatever you do, don't be tempted to stage some outlandish stunt to grab your employer's attention. Don't be the guy who spent his last £500 on a billboard asking for a job. Or the girl who built her CV in Lego. Or that person who had the company's name tattooed on their forehead. Be a calm, assured, intelligent candidate and pretty soon things will go your way.

HOW CAN I STAY SANE IN A WORLD GONE MAD?

THERE HAS NEVER been a better time to be a human being. It's important to remember that. Amidst the doom and gloom of culture wars, and the climate emergency, and the regressive tendencies of our politics, it's tempting to see our world with negativity and despondency. But the truth is, there's never been a better time to be alive. This is not to suggest that everything, everywhere is marvellous, but at a high level, on average, things are more marvellous than ever before.

Since the fifties, for example, child mortality has plummeted, while over the same period literacy and schooling rates have boomed. The number of people living in poverty today is a quarter of what it was in 1980. Meanwhile, GDP per capita has nearly tripled.

Challenging social issues remain, of course. For all our economic and scientific progress, we've yet to abolish oppression and discrimination. But still, in relative terms, things are better. In all but the more traditional and conservative countries, LGBT rights are more established than ever before, female suffrage is near-universal and laws protecting minority ethnic groups are stronger. Injustice, unfairness, violence and wrongdoing persist – I really must stress that – and we must campaign and work harder to overcome these grotesque inequalities. But even the staunchest, most committed pessimist must submit to the statistical reality that life today is the best it's ever been.

What's even more exciting about our progress isn't just that it helps lift today's humans out of poverty and pain, but that it also speeds up change for the next generation. Progress begets progress; one technological breakthrough accelerates the arrival of the next. 'We live in a moment packed with new possibilities,' say Ian Goldin and Chris Kutarna (authors of the brilliant *Age of Discovery*). 'And we've never been better equipped to seize them.'

And yet, in spite of all this, one perplexing curiosity remains. Namely, why is it that we're not happier? The vast majority of us now live longer, healthier, more comfortable lives. The threat of suffering a violent death, or being hungry, or having to go to war are fractions of what they once were, but no one, it seems, has told our mental health. Global cases of depression, for example, rose by nearly 20 per cent between 2005 and 2015. While, around the world, roughly 280 million of us struggle with anxiety disorders.

Work is a big part of this. As we saw earlier, the mismatch between our soaring expectations and the ever-diminishing realities of modern jobs is a huge driver of discontent. It's the tidal flow on which so many of my generation drift along. But other factors are at play, too. Our world is safer and more prosperous, but this progress hasn't been free of charge; there have been costs and by-products. The natural world has shouldered much of this burden, but so have we.

In pursuing growth, modernisation and a dream of 'more', humankind has paid a heavy price. Not just in terms of the most extreme measures – the depression and anxiety rates – but the modern world has also played havoc with our weight, and our sex lives, and our self-esteem. It's hardly surprising, for example, that while 35 per cent of Americans report struggling with their sleep, in pre-industrial societies in Africa and Bolivia that figure approaches 0 per cent. Indeed, according to researchers from UCLA, several of these communities (including the San people in Namibia and the Tsimané from Bolivia) don't even have a word for insomnia.

Of course, much of our current strife (or the potential for it) is hardwired. Ever since we were scratching around in caves and jungles, our species has been defined by competition – for food, for shelter, for partners. And wherever you find competition, anxiety and stress are never far behind.

The nature of modern competition is very different, of course. Now we fight for money, power and fame, rather than for food or our lives. But that doesn't mean it's any less impactful on our psyches. In some ways – as with our expectations of work – the intangibility of what we're competing for makes it even more detrimental. The competition never ends. Winning one victory, say for a career promotion or house purchase, simply leads to another battle, for a bigger Instagram following, a shinier car or a skinnier waist. It's as though we're never finished, never done wanting 'more' than those around us.

It's also the case that (depressingly) much of modern commerce is predicated on our misery. As someone who used to sell advertising, I can say categorically that the vast majority of what passes for 'marketing' is intended to make the consumer unhappy. First you make them unhappy by manufacturing an impossible standard of beauty, or health, or popularity. Then, once they're miserable, you suggest your product as the answer. Except it isn't. It can't be. It doesn't matter how many yoghurts you drink, your life will never be as carefree and smiley as the one in the advert. It doesn't matter how many times you use the shampoo, your hair will never be that shiny. It doesn't matter how many pairs of Calvin Kleins you buy, you'll never look like that picture of Kendall Jenner. Because even Kendall Jenner doesn't look like that picture of Kendall Jenner all of the time. No one does. The vast majority of social media is airbrushed, made-up, fake, created on a computer by nerds in a dark, smelly room. But that doesn't matter, because as long as we're still miserable, there are still opportunities to flog us alternative 'fixes'. Maybe if you had a new washing machine you'd be happy? Maybe if you ate more cereal bars you'd be enough? Or if you had expensive aftershave? Or a newer phone?

Naturally, the advertising industry (and the folks who use it) isn't the only one profiting from our pain. The primary premise of news media, for example, is fear. We know this; that news stories about famine, war, death, rape and murder are awarded the greatest prominence isn't new. 'If it bleeds, it leads,' the cliché goes. And we also know what ingesting a near-constant diet of negativity and panic does for our well-being. It makes us worry about the news itself, yes – the wars, the hurricanes, the impending Armageddons – but watching the news also heightens other, independent fears – about our weight, our work, our partners. Pretty soon, all of this scaremongering, fear and discord changes how we see the world. 'It becomes,' as sociologist David Altheide says, 'a way of looking at life.'

It's the same with social media, too. Not only does social media cause depression, anxiety, low mood and low self-esteem, often its business model is dependent on it. The social media companies need us to be discontented, because that's what drives our consumption. Think about it. If we were all delighted with our lives, content with our appearances and happy with our holiday choices, why would we spend any time gawping at Instagram? If we were all comfortable in our own skin and satisfied with our relationships, why would we bother following influencers?

Perhaps, you might argue, voyeurism and gossip are natural human tendencies, and that, even without social media, we'd still be interested in the lives of others. And to some extent you'd be right. According to the evolutionary psychologist Robin Dunbar, humankind's fascination with gossip is so old and entrenched that it can be traced back to the grooming rituals we engaged in as primates. What's different about modern gossip, though, is that it's a lonely business. Chinwagging with a fellow monkey while they pull ticks out of your fur is a communal, bonding activity. Scrolling through other folks' lives on social media while sitting on the loo isn't. We're not conversing, learning or discussing while we do it. Mostly we're sitting alone, cursing how wretched our lives seem versus the ones on our screens.

'But social media helps us to keep connected.' No it doesn't. It allows us to *message* each other, sure. And it also enables us to gorge on other people's successes, talents and lives. But it absolutely does not connect us. In fact, as before, a collective, societal disconnection is central to the social business model. That's how they make their money, that's the whole point. They need us to be disconnected so that we keep on using them. Because if we all had meaningful friendships, deep connections and profound conversations, then the need for messaging apps and instant communication would largely disappear. We wouldn't need it. Just like our ancient ancestors in, say, the eighties didn't need it.

I know all this might sound a bit hippy-dippy, but it's also true. And you needn't take it from me. In their unguarded moments, even the social media bosses themselves admit that their businesses depend on the darkest human emotions. 'Social networks do best when they tap into one of the seven deadly sins,' says LinkedIn founder Reid Hoffman. 'LinkedIn is greed. With Facebook, it's vanity, and how people choose to present themselves to their friends.'

Recognising all of this – that there's more to our collective unhappiness, anxiety and drift than purely work – is really important. Our careers are an unquestionably large piece of the puzzle, but there are others. And just as we have to be intentional, considered and effortful about sorting out the jobs bit, we must do the same with this stuff. We have to accept that much of the modern world is designed to make us mad and sad, and commit to protecting ourselves from it. Otherwise there's a danger (quite a considerable one) that you'll fix your career by finding fulfilling work, only to discover that you remain discontented, unbalanced and directionless.

HOW TO STAY SANE

Since my breakdown, the question I get asked more than any other is 'How did you cure yourself?' And, depending on the context, I'll give one of two answers.

If it's at the end of a corporate gig and the boss (who's invariably spent the whole talk staring at his phone, resenting his attendance) has decided to feign interest in mental health by asking a question, then I go for something short and pithy: 'Drink less, exercise more, delete Instagram' . . . that sort of thing.

Under any other circumstances, though, I'll be honest. I'll say that while I'm a lot, lot better than four years ago, I'm not 'cured' of my anxiety disorder; that I never will be and that realising this has been an essential part of recovery. In fact, until I recognised that I'd never get 100 per cent better, I couldn't get better at all. Instead, I was trapped in a terrible search for the one thing, the elixir, that would fix me completely and immediately. Perhaps meditation would return me to my pre-breakdown state? Maybe obsessive exercise was the answer? Maybe pills, or drink, or drugs, or self-harm were what I needed?

In reality, of course, it was a variety of things – repeated calmly, over a long period of time – which put me on the path towards mental peace, but I haven't been 'cured'. And I'm just convinced – totally, utterly convinced – that the things which got me out of the deepest, darkest depths of my mental health problem, are the exact same things which would have stopped me having one in the first place. For me they were a lifeline, an escape slide; for you they might be an insurance policy. And regardless of whether you're stuck in a job you hate, or moving towards one you think you might love, or out of work altogether, I'd strongly encourage you to consider the below.

We have to fix our jobs and careers – of course we do – but this is also an opportunity to work on some of the other things that contribute to our malaise, too.

BOOZE LESS

It is a truth universally acknowledged that humans, in worrying times, must be in want of a beer. Or wine. Or, in the case of my wife, a cocktail in a can. It's been this way for millennia. Discoveries of clay vessels in northern China, for example, suggest that humans have been using booze as balm for well over 9,000 years. And, although those ancient Chinese drinkers weren't tucking into a pint of Carlsberg or a glass of Prosecco, their motivations were no different from the thousands of us who turned to alcohol during the coronavirus pandemic (liquor sales in March 2020 were 54 per cent higher than those in that same week in 2019). Put simply, when the world is cold, scary, uncertain and panicked, most of us reach for the Jacob's Creek.

There are a number of reasons why this isn't a good idea; and why, particularly if you're having a rubbish time at work or out of work, I'd caution against self-medication.

The first is to do with brain chemistry and the irritating fact that alcohol and mental health are sworn enemies. I say 'irritating' because the idea of coming home after a hard day hating work and cracking open a cold one, Homer Simpson-style, sounds rather lovely. But in reality, alcohol's effects on the brain are profound, broadly negative and not quite what you might think. Ask most folks how booze affects the brain and they'll doubtless tell you that it depends on the drink in question. Accepted wisdom has it that some drinks are depressants (whiskey, gin, etc.), whereas others are fun, stimulating, pick-me-ups (champagne, espresso Martinis and so forth). But in reality, all ethanol is *both* a stimulant and a depressant. When we drink, our brains are flooded with things like dopamine, serotonin and (later on, after a drinking session) endorphins. These have the effect of making us happy, relaxed and without inhibition. But at the same time, alcohol slows and impairs the function of other neurotransmitters (which is why we slur and stagger when we're drunk).

Combined, these opposing forces throw off the delicately calibrated, finely balanced chemical make-up of our brains. And this, sadly, is always bad news for mood, anxiety and self-esteem.

Which is to say nothing of alcohol's effects on our weight gain (and subsequently our self-esteem). Or sleep for that matter. You might think that you fall asleep quicker when you've had a few drinks, and you'd be right. But you also wake up much more throughout the night and the quality of the sleep you enjoy is much lower.

> Getting a good night's sleep is always a key element of human well-being, but this is particularly true during periods of high stress or uncertainty.

What we want is that delicious, deep, restful, restorative 'rapid eye movement' sleep that experts are always telling us about. And when you're drunk (or even just a pinch pissed), you get much less of that. Alcohol sleep is a thin, brittle, shallow, almost staccato affair.

This is not an argument for sobriety, mind you. I did that for six months back when everything first went pear-shaped, and while I certainly didn't miss the hangovers, it wasn't sustainable. I have nothing but admiration for people who can attend a wedding, and chat and dance without getting drunk – I'm just not one of them. So in place of teetotalism, now I have rules. I try never to drink from Monday through to Thursday and, even when I do booze, I try not to drink past the point that I think I'll get a hangover. Obviously, this is not a perfect science – I get it wrong all the time. In fact, I got it horrifically wrong last weekend, but I do find that having a framework and being mindful of how much I drink somehow reduces it. I'm sure it'll be the same for you, particularly if you feel yourself drifting through a job you hate or if you're out of work altogether. As we saw earlier, paddling out of career creek is always hard work, but it'll be much, much easier if you're not spending your evenings getting hammered and your mornings hanging over.

EXERCISE MORE

Before my life fell apart I was a committed couch potato. In the years leading up to my breakdown, I can scarcely recall a single jog, swim or trip to the gym. And while, as the cupboard under our stairs will attest, I'm very good at buying all sorts of sports kit and equipment, I was never any good at actually using any of it.

That all changed after my breakdown. It had to. With anxious thoughts swirling around my head and adrenaline coursing constantly through my veins, exercise became a necessity. It became one of the few things I could do to quieten the noise in my head and make use of the hormones in my blood. At the start, I wasn't very good at it. In fact – I might as well be honest – I'm still no good at it. In the four years I've been exercising regularly I've shaved a paltry two minutes off my five-km run time. And my bench pressing limit remains roughly equivalent to an 80-year-old lady's. But that isn't the point. I don't exercise to get better, or bigger, or svelter. I exercise because I have to; because it lifts my mood, makes me feel purposeful and distracts me from whatever's gone wrong. And I'm not alone. The research is very clear here – exercising just three times a week for a minimum of 30 minutes has been shown to better mood, reduce anxiety and improve sleep.

It's also something you can do. That sounds an obvious point, but the most unsettling thing about a mental health problem, or drifting in an uncertain career, or a spell of unemployment, is the lack of control. Thrust into a situation or circumstance beyond your influence, it's easy to feel lost and forlorn – like a kite in a hurricane, or a cork on the ocean, or a tourist in Leicester Square.

Exercising – particularly when you don't want to – helps to overcome all that. It's a positive, wilful action, a way to wrestle back control. It's a lever to pull – *your* lever. No one can stop you lacing up your trainers or dusting off your swimming goggles. And when you do it, you feel fantastic. The exertion, endorphins and serotonin make your body feel taut and toned, while the fact that you did something when you didn't have to boosts your self-esteem: 'Maybe I'm not such a useless, podgy schlub after all.'

Of course, as with so many things, it's important not to become obsessive about exercise. If you can't play tennis this evening or swim tomorrow, you'll be absolutely fine. But if you can, then do.

CHALLENGE YOUR THOUGHTS

We've spoken a few times about how scatty the human mind is, but it's such an important point that I'm hoping you'll forgive me reiterating that, while our brains are big, beautiful, powerful and predictive, they're also capable of churning out total garbage.

It took a breakdown for me to realise this. Before that, like most people, I assumed that the thoughts in my head were logical. If my brain said that I didn't like tomatoes, or that I couldn't stand Coldplay, or that I was a useless piece of shit, I tended to believe it. Then I went through four years of intense CBT and my opinion changed. I couldn't not change my mind. Because within the first few sessions it became glaringly apparent that lots of the thoughts in my head (maybe 70 per cent of them) were utter rubbish. There wasn't any logic to them or evidence to support them. They were just thoughts – brain farts – with little to no validity and which crumbled under even the slightest interrogation.

'You'll never sleep again,' my brain said. Oh really? It's just that you've said that a million times since my breakdown and, while there have been bouts of insomnia, at some point I always sleep again.

'You'll be like this forever.' Will I? Will I really be like this forever? Because you said the same thing last month, but then it got better. That wedding you said I'd never be able to go to, that meeting you told me I'd fluff – all of that went just fine. So maybe it'll be bad for a while, but it will always improve. And so on.

CBT has been, unquestionably, one of the largest, strongest pillars of my recovery. And while I'm not suggesting that every drifter needs a big, formal process of therapy, the basic principles do have powerful applications within the context of career creek.

The framework for CBT starts from the premise that our thoughts, feelings and behaviours are all tightly interconnected. If we have an anxious or depressed thought, the theory goes, that leads to anxious or depressed feelings in our bodies, which in turn leads us to behave in certain ways. It might mean, for example, that you begin avoiding social situations, or start drinking heavily, or stay in a job you hate. Then, because you've exhibited the feelings and behaviours, your brain takes that as evidence that the original thought was correct. Pretty soon, an ever-tightening knot or loop begins to form. The thoughts lead to the feelings and behaviours, which result in even more thoughts. And on it goes.

The idea of CBT is to prevent that process from happening by arresting, isolating and challenging the thoughts with logic and evidence before they can become feelings or behaviours. It doesn't aim to stop the thoughts rocking up (because that's impossible); it just tries to prevent them becoming feelings or behaviours. There are a few ways to do this, but most often it's about asking questions. The two most pertinent ones being: 'What is the real likelihood of this thought coming true?' and 'Even if the thought does come true, how bad would it really be? What's the worst, worst-case scenario?' At the start, this process of isolating and challenging your thoughts is very manual, but it quickly becomes automatic.

And after a few weeks, what you discover is that the vast majority of scary and depressing thoughts are both less likely and far less severe than you'd originally guessed.

None of this is about 'thinking yourself happy' or becoming some irritating perma-optimist. And it's also not claiming that, to borrow from *The Lego Movie*, 'everything is awesome', because there are some things in life that are worthy of our worry and despair: climate change, global pandemics, and so forth. It's just that lots of the thoughts in our heads aren't those things. They're not real, tangible, evidenced-based problems. Instead they're made-up, invented, unevidenced and illogical bullshit. And that's as true for negative and anxious thoughts about work, as it is for anything else. Where's the evidence that you'll never find a job you love? Or that you've left it too late? Or that you'll be unemployed forever? There isn't any. In fact, as we've seen throughout this book, the logic suggests the complete opposite.

ASK FOR HELP

Without doubt, the most profound discovery of the past few years has been how wonderful humans are. Not always, of course. Even on the warmest, sunniest summer day a decent chunk of our humanity remains steadfastly grumpy, irritable and quick to chide. But on the whole, in the round, averaged out, other people are brilliant.

We saw this in action throughout the coronavirus pandemic. Confined to our quarters, lonely and scared, we witnessed humankind rise to greatness in its most caring and generous form. We saw nurses and doctors risk their lives to help save other people's. We saw delivery drivers pound through the night to make sure the shelves were stacked. We saw strangers bring their neighbours food, and medicine, and smiles, and conversations through the letterbox. We saw a million people volunteer for the NHS scheme – three times what they had expected. And we saw, above all, the collective genius of mankind come together to defeat the virus with science and vaccines. Not for selfish or greedy or commercial motivations, but because, at our most essential, we're a species built on empathy, compassion and kindness.

Courtesy of my breakdown, I've had something of a head start in realising all of this. Prior to that, like lots of folks, I had a slightly dim view of humanity. I saw us having horrific wars, and biffing carbon into the atmosphere, and being grim to each other, and assumed that our default setting was 'horrible'. But then I started asking for help – I started *needing* help – and very quickly I found the opposite to be true. Friends were fantastic, doctors were determined, my employers couldn't have been kinder. There were taxi drivers who gave me free fares when they spotted me crying, and a lady in A&E who bought me a Snickers because I looked glum after a panic attack, and my boss who let me work from home three days a week. 'Whatever you need,' they all said. 'Just let us know.'

The reason I bring these things up is because you can't fix your career on your own. You need help – quite a bit of help actually. Whether it's your friends helping you to define your 'why', or your family supporting you through lean times, or someone offering advice on your side hustle, you're going to need other people. That might seem challenging or embarrassing, but have faith that it isn't. The very moment you ask for help and advice, you'll be amazed by how people respond. They'll help you, nurture you, guide you and promote you. They'll read your CV for you, or connect you with their friend, or get you in for work experience. It always pays to be clear about what help you want, mind you. And you also have to be prepared to be persistent. But in my experience, once you nudge someone towards kindness they very rarely resist. All you need to do is ask them and they'll help push you along in your quest to find fulfilling work.

And you will find it.

A fulfilling, marvellous, immersive and purposeful career is out there waiting for you. Obtaining it, as we've seen, will require deliberate effort, hard work and compromise. You'll have to work out what you want from life and what you hate. You'll have to chew through hundreds of job descriptions. You'll have to commit to writing brilliant, deeply researched CVs and covering letters. You'll have to figure out whether a proactive approach would work best and whether a side hustle or starting your own business is the answer. You might even have to move through a spell of unemployment with composure. And, above all, you'll need to stay calm.

All of which might sound a bit daunting and difficult, and at times it will be. But I promise it will be less difficult – let alone less depressing – than moving through your career without ever finding rhythm, comfort and enjoyment. Plus, whatever difficulty you do experience will be temporary. In total it took me two years to move from hating my career so much that I had a breakdown to approaching Sunday evenings with a sense of excitement and possibility. You might get there quicker, or it might take longer. But you can get there – I promise that, I *know* that. After all, one way or another, everyone can escape career creek; all they need is the right paddle.

NOTES

1 WELCOME TO CAREER CREEK

Baum, G., 1982. *The Priority of Labour. A Commentary on Laborem exercens, Encyclical Letter of Pope John Paul II*. New York/Ramsey, Paulist Press.

Chicago Tribune, 5 Sep. 1994. The true meaning of our labor. Retrieved from https://www.chicagotribune.com/news/ct-xpm-1994-09-05-9409050052-story.html.

Gallup, 2016. How millennials want to work and live. Retrieved from https://www.gallup.com/workplace/238073/millennials-work-live.aspx.

Graeber, D., 2018. *Bullshit Jobs: A theory*. Allen Lane.

Graeber, D., 2013. On the phenomenon of bullshit jobs: A work rant. *Strike*. Retrieved from https://theanarchistlibrary.org/library/david-graeber-on-the-phenomenon-of-bullshit-jobs-a-work-rant.

Udemy for Business, 2016. 2016 Udemy workplace boredom study. Retrieved from https://research.udemy.com/wp-content/uploads/2016/10/2016-Udemy-Workplace-Boredom-Study.pdf.

2 WHY ARE WE DRIFTING?

Adkins, A., 12 May 2016. Millennials: The job-hopping generation. Gallup. Retrieved from https://www.gallup.com/workplace/236474/millennials-job-hopping-generation.aspx.

Bouxsein, K. J., Roane, H. S. and Harper, T., 2011. Evaluating the separate and combined effects of positive and negative reinforcement on task compliance. *Journal of Applied Behavior Analysis*, *44*(1), pp. 175–9.

Brickman, P., Coates, D. and Janoff-Bulman, R., 1978. Lottery winners and accident victims: Is happiness relative? *Journal of Personality and Social Psychology*, *36*(8), p. 917.

Bristowe. M., 12 Aug. 2014. The millennial mandate. *HuffPost*. Retrieved from https://www.huffpost.com/entry/the-millennial-mandate_b_6287948.

Collinson, P., 13 Oct. 2018. UK millennials' costs among EU's highest – but pay lags behind. *Guardian*. Retrieved from https://www.theguardian.com/money/2018/oct/13/uk-millennials-costs-eu-pay-rent-transport-grocery-revolut.

Deloitte, 2019. The Deloitte global millennial survey 2019. Retrieved from https://www2.deloitte.com/content/dam/Deloitte/global/Documents/About-Deloitte/deloitte-2019-millennial-survey.pdf.

Deloitte, 2020. Deloitte survey reveals that millennials and Gen Z view the COVID-19 pandemic as an opportunity to reset and take action. Retrieved from https://www2.deloitte.com/ua/en/pages/press-room/press-release/2020/millenial-survey-2020.html.

Deloitte, 2021. A call for accountability and action. Retrieved from https://www2.deloitte.com/content/dam/Deloitte/global/Documents/2021-deloitte-global-millennial-survey-report.pdf.

Forness, S. R., Kavale, K. A., Blum, I. M. and Lloyd, J. W., 1997. Mega-analysis of meta-analyses. *Teaching Exceptional Children*, *29*(6), p. 4.

Graeber, D., 2013. On the phenomenon of bullshit jobs: A work rant. *Strike*. Retrieved from https://theanarchistlibrary.org/library/david-graeber-on-the-phenomenon-of-bullshit-jobs-a-work-rant.

Grzywacz, J. G., Segel-Karpas, D. and Lachman, M. E., 2016. Workplace exposures and cognitive function during adulthood: Evidence from National Survey of Midlife Development and the O* NET. *Journal of Occupational and Environmental Medicine, 58*(6), pp. 535–41.

Harari, Y. N., 2015. *Sapiens: A brief history of humankind*. Vintage.

Indeed, 22 Sep. 2015. Who actively looks for jobs today? Answer: Almost everyone [blog]. Retrieved from https://blog.indeed.co.uk/2015/09/22/who-actively-looks-for-jobs-today-answer-almost-everyone-new-data.

Jobvite, 2018. 2018 Job seeker nation study. Retrieved from https://www.jobvite.com/wp-content/uploads/2018/04/2018_Job_Seeker_Nation_Study.pdf.

Kessler, S., 11 Oct. 2017. Gen X was as entitled and unmanageable as millennials are, based on commentary of the '90s. Quartz at Work. Retrieved from https://qz.com/work/1070139/millennials-are-no-harder-to-manage-than-generation-x-according-to-the-commentary-of-the-1990s.

Kreun, A., 8 June 2016. Misguided Advice: What To Do With Millennials. LinkedIn. Retrieved from https://www.linkedin.com/pulse/misguided-advice-what-do-millennials-michael-stewart.

Lifton, R. J., 1989. *Thought Reform and the Psychology of Totalism: A study of 'brainwashing' in China*. University of North Carolina Press.

Ma, H. H., 2010. Comparison of the relative effectiveness of different kinds of reinforcers: A PEM approach. *The Behavior Analyst Today, 10*(3–4), p. 398.

National Institute of Mental Health, n.d. Any anxiety disorder. Retrieved from https://www.nimh.nih.gov/health/statistics/any-anxiety-disorder.

National Institute of Mental Health, Oct. 2021. Major depression. Retrieved from https://www.nimh.nih.gov/health/statistics/major-depression.

Newsweek, 6 May 1994. Generalizations X. Retrieved from https://www.news-week.com/generalizations-x-189124.

O'Connor, S., 23 Feb. 2018. Millennials poorer than previous generations, data show. *Financial Times*. Retrieved from https://www.ft.com/content/81343d9e-187b-11e8-9e9c-25c814761640.

Office for National Statistics, 21 Jan. 2021. Average household income, UK: Financial year 2020. Retrieved from https://www.ons.gov.uk/peoplepopulationandcommunity/personalandhouseholdfinances/incomeandwealth/bulletins/householddisposableincomeandinequality/financialyear2020.

Ortiz-Ospina, E., 11 Dec. 2019. Is there a loneliness epidemic? Our WorldInData.org. Retrieved from https://ourworldindata.org/loneliness-epidemic.

R. A., 21 Aug. 2013. On 'bullshit jobs'. *The Economist*. Retrieved from https://www.economist.com/free-exchange/2013/08/21/on-bullshit-jobs.

Roberts, B. W., Edmonds, G. and Grijalva, E., 2010. It is developmental me, not generation me: Developmental changes are more important than generational changes in narcissism – commentary on Trzesniewski & Donnellan. *Perspectives on Psychological Science*, 5(1), pp. 97–102.

Sarner, M., 9 Oct. 2018. The age of envy: How to be happy when everyone else's life looks perfect. *Guardian*. Retrieved from https://www.theguardian.com/lifeandstyle/2018/oct/09/age-envy-be-happy-everyone-else-perfect-social-media.

Schwantes, M., 30 May 2018. Research confirms what we all suspected. Millennials in the workplace are not that different from other generations. Inc. Retrieved from https://www.inc.com/marcel-schwantes/research-confirms-what-we-all-suspected-millennials-in-workplace-are-not-that-different-from-other-generations.html.

Sinek, S., n.d. The millennial question [video]. Retrieved from https://simon-sinek.com/discover/the-millennial-question.

Stein, J., 20 May 2013. Millennials: The me me me generation. *Time*. Retrieved from https://time.com/247/millennials-the-me-me-me-generation.

Twenge, J. M., Konrath, S., Foster, J. D., Keith Campbell, W. and Bushman, B. J., 2008. Egos inflating over time: A cross-temporal meta-analysis of the Narcissistic Personality Inventory. *Journal of Personality*, *76*(4), pp. 875–902.

The World Bank, 2011. Adjusted net national income per capita (current US$). Retrieved from https://data.worldbank.org/indicator/NY.ADJ.NNTY.PC.CD?end=2019&start=2019&view=bar.

Young Invincibles, 13 Jan. 2017. The financial health of young America. Retrieved from https://younginvincibles.org/financial-health-young-america.

3 HAVE I LEFT IT TOO LATE?

Conn, D., 19 Nov. 2018. More than 500 footballers may have lost up to £1bn due to bad advice. *Guardian*. Retrieved from https://www.theguardian.com/football/2018/nov/19/more-than-500-footballers-may-have-lost-up-to-1bn-due-to-bad-advice.

Earhart, Amelia, official website of, 2021. Quotes by Amelia Earhart. Retrieved from https://ameliaearhart.com/index.php/quotes.

Fields, D., 21 Mar. 2018. Aden + Anais and founder Raegan Moya-Jones part ways. *Forbes*. Retrieved from https://www.forbes.com/sites/mergermarket/2018/03/21/aden-anais-and-founder-raegan-moya-jones-part-ways/?sh=5405c64c7f20.

4 HOW CAN I OVERCOME CAREER FEAR?

Achor, S., Reece, A., Kellerman, G. R. and Robichaux, A., 6 Nov. 2018. 9 out of 10 people are willing to earn less money to do more-meaningful work. *Harvard Business Review*, *96*(6), pp. 82–9.

American Psychological Association, 2020. Enmeshment. APA Dictionary of Psychology. Retrieved from https://dictionary.apa.org/enmeshment.

Giddens, A., 1991. *Modernity and Self-identity*. Stanford University Press.

Gollwitzer, P. M. and Sheeran, P., 2006. Implementation intentions and goal achievement: A meta-analysis of effects and processes. *Advances in Experimental Social Psychology*, *38*(6), pp. 69–119.

Hoffman, R., 10 Jun. 2020. ABZ planning. Greylock. Retrieved from https://greylock.com/greymatter/reid-hoffman-abzplanning.

Sandberg, S., 2013. *Lean In: Women, work, and the will to lead*. WH Allen.

Sivers, D., Jul. 2010. Keep your goals to yourself [video]. TED. Retrieved from https://www.ted.com/talks/derek_sivers_keep_your_goals_to_yourself?language=en.

Zak, P. J., 2017. The neuroscience of trust. *Harvard Business Review*, *95*(1), pp. 84–90.

5 WHAT JOB SHOULD I DO?

de Bernières, L., 1998. *Captain Corelli's Mandolin*. Vintage, ch. 47.

Kahneman, D., 2012. *Thinking, Fast and Slow*. Penguin.

6 HOW SHOULD I DEFINE SUCCESS?

Niemiec, C. P., Ryan, R. M. and Deci, E. L., 2009. The path taken: Consequences of attaining intrinsic and extrinsic aspirations in post-college life. *Journal of Research in Personality*, *43*(3), pp. 291–306.

Tolstoy, L., 17 Jul. 2009. *A Confession*. Merchant Books.

7 DO I NEED A SIDE HUSTLE?

AWeber, 2020. The 2020 small business email marketing statistics report. Retrieved from https://www.aweber.com/2020-report.

Blomfield, T., Apr. 2018. Monzo staff weekly Q&A. Monzo. Retrieved from https://community.monzo.com/t/monzo-staff-weekly-q-a-tom-blomfield-ceo/35721/69.

Hil, A., 15 Feb. 2021. 'We were made for this': the women starting businesses in lockdown. *Guardian*. Retrieved from https://www.theguardian.com/world/2021/feb/15/the-women-starting-businesses-in-lockdown-the-upside.

Hoffman, R., n.d. Learn from every 'no' [podcast]. Masters of Scale. Retrieved from https://mastersofscale.com/tristan-walker-beauty-of-a-bad-idea.

Navasky, V., 29 Sep. 1996. Tomorrow never knows. *New York Times Magazine*. Retrieved from https://www.nytimes.com/1996/09/29/magazine/tomorrow-never-knows.html.

Partington, R., 28 Jun. 2019. Gig economy in Britain doubles, accounting for 4.7 million workers. *Guardian*. Retrieved from https://www.theguardian.com/business/2019/jun/28/gig-economy-in-britain-doubles-accounting-for-47-million-workers.

Paynter Jacket Co., n.d. How it works. Retrieved from https://paynterjacket.com/pages/how-it-works.

Rottenberg, L., n.d. The next silicon valley [podcast]. Masters of Scale. Retrieved from https://mastersofscale.com/linda-rottenberg-the-next-silicon-valley.

Sillars, J., 17 May 2021. COVID-19: People working from home in UK more than doubled as pandemic struck – but at what cost? Sky News. Retrieved from https://news.sky.com/story/covid-19-8-4-million-were-working-from-home-last-year-as-pandemic-struck-12309068.

8 WILL I SURVIVE A SPELL OF UNEMPLOYMENT?

Bilton, N., 2014. *Hatching Twitter: A true story of money, power, friendship, and betrayal*. Portfolio.

Ford, H., 20 Aug. 2000. Inside the Actors Studio, season 6, episode 13.

Glassdoor, 2018. 65 HR & recruiting stats for 2018. Retrieved from https://resources.glassdoor.com/65-hr-recruiting-stats-2018.html?Channel=blog&_gl=1*13lm2ix*_ga*MTYwODE1NjYzNi4xNjM0NzE1NDY4*_ga_RC95P MVB3H*MTYzNDcxNTQ2OC4xLjAuMTYzNDcxNTQ2OC42MA.

Herbig, B., Dragano, N. and Angerer, P., 2013. Health in the long-term unemployed. *Deutsches Ärzteblatt International*, *110*(23–24), pp. 413–19.

Kroft, K., Lange, F. and Notowidigdo, M. J., 2013. Duration dependence and labor market conditions: Evidence from a field experiment. *The Quarterly Journal of Economics*, *128*(3), pp. 1123–67.

Krueger, A. B., Mueller, A., Davis, S. J. and Şahin, A., 2011. Job search, emotional well-being, and job finding in a period of mass unemployment: Evidence from high frequency longitudinal data [with comments and discussion]. *Brookings Papers on Economic Activity*, pp. 1–81.

Lally, P., Van Jaarsveld, C. H., Potts, H. W. and Wardle, J., 2010. How are habits formed: Modelling habit formation in the real world. *European Journal of Social Psychology*, *40*(6), pp. 998–1009.

Office for National Statistics, 14 Sep. 2021. Employment in the UK: September 2021. Retrieved from https://www.ons.gov.uk/employmentandlabourmarket/peopleinwork/employmentandemployeetypes/bulletins/employmentintheuk/september2021.

Patt, A. and Zeckhauser, R., 2000. Action bias and environmental decisions. *Journal of Risk and Uncertainty*, *21*(1), pp. 45–72.

PricewaterhouseCoopers LLP, 2018. How will automation impact jobs? Retrieved from https://www.pwc.co.uk/services/economics/insights/the-impact-of-automation-on-jobs.html.

Trafton, A., 16 Nov. 2017. Stress can lead to risky decisions. MIT News. Retrieved from https://news.mit.edu/2017/stress-can-lead-risky-decisions -1116.

Ward, M., 29 Jan. 2017. 5 things you didn't know about Oprah Winfrey. *Vogue*. Retrieved from https://www.vogue.com/article/oprah-winfrey-5-things-you-didnt-know.

9 HOW CAN I ACTUALLY GET THE JOB?

Adler, L., 29 Feb. 2016. New survey reveals 85% of all jobs are filled via networking. LinkedIn. Retrieved from https://www.linkedin.com/pulse/new-survey-reveals-85-all-jobs-filled-via-networking-lou-adler.

Kawalkowska, M., 24 Jan. 2019. These stats prove the importance of follow-up emails [blog]. Woodpecker. Retrieved from https://woodpecker.co/blog/follow-up-statistics.

Kooti, F., Aiello, L. M., Grbovic, M., Lerman, K. and Mantrach, A., 2015. Evolution of conversations in the age of email overload. *Proceedings of the 24th International Conference on World Wide Web*, pp. 603–13.

Ladders, 2018. Eye-tracking study. Retrieved from https://www.theladders.com /static/images/basicSite/pdfs/TheLadders-EyeTracking-StudyC2.pdf.

McKeon, K., 28 Apr. 2020. 5 personal branding tips for your job search. The Manifest. Retrieved from https://themanifest.com/digital-marketing/5-personal-branding-tips-job-search.

Qu, L., 7 Nov. 2019. 99% of Fortune 500 companies use Applicant Tracking Systems. Jobscan. Retrieved from https://www.jobscan.co/blog/99-percent-fortune-500-ats.

Reynolds, B., n.d. What is an applicant tracking system, and how does it affect my job applications? FlexJobs. Retrieved from https://www.flexjobs.com/job -search-career-advice/what_is_an_applicant_tracking_system_and_how_ does_it_affect_my_job_applications.

Smith, M., 10 Apr. 2017. Disgracebook: One in five employers have turned down a candidate because of social media. YouGov. Retrieved from https://yougov.co.uk/topics/politics/articles-reports/2017/04/10/disgracebook-one-five-employers-have-turned-down-c.

Wong, J. S. and Penner, A. M., 2016. Gender and the returns to attractiveness. *Research in Social Stratification and Mobility*, *44*, pp. 113–23.

10 HOW CAN I STAY SANE IN A WORLD GONE MAD?

Altheide, D., 2002. *Creating Fear: News and the construction of crisis*. Routledge.

Choi, K. W., Zheutlin, A. B., Karlson, R. A., Wang, M. J., Dunn, E. C., Stein, M. B., Karlson, E. W. and Smoller, J. W., 2020. Physical activity offsets genetic risk for incident depression assessed via electronic health records in a biobank cohort study. *Depression and Anxiety*, *37*(2), pp. 106–14.

Division of Population Health, 2 May 2017. Short sleep duration among US adults. National Center for Chronic Disease Prevention and Health Promotion. Retrieved from https://www.cdc.gov/sleep/data_statistics.html.

Dunbar, R., 1997. *Grooming, Gossip and the Evolution of Language*. Harvard University Press.

Goldin, I. and Kutarna, C., 15 May 2016. We're living in an age full of possibilities. So why do so many of us feel like losers? *Guardian*. Retrieved from https://www.theguardian.com/commentisfree/2016/may/15/future-progress-renaissance-internet-europe.

Meyer, R., 9 May 2016. The seven deadly social networks. *The Atlantic*. Retrieved from https://www.theatlantic.com/technology/archive/2016/05/the-seven-deadly-social-networks/480897.

NielsenIQ, 7 May 2020. Rebalancing the 'Covid-19 effect' on alcohol sales. Retrieved from https://nielseniq.com/global/en/insights/analysis/2020/rebalancing-the-covid-19-effect-on-alcohol-sales.

O'Neill, A., 9 Sep. 2019. Child mortality in the United Kingdom 1800–2020. Statista. Retrieved from https://www.statista.com/statistics/1041714/united-kingdom-all-time-child-mortality-rate.

Passos, G. S., Poyares, D., Santana, M. G., D'Aurea, C. V. R., Youngstedt, S. D., Tufik, S. and de Mello, M. T., 2011. Effects of moderate aerobic exercise training on chronic primary insomnia. *Sleep Medicine*, *12*(10), pp. 1018–27.

Roser, M., 2013. Economic growth. Published online at OurWorldInData.org. Retrieved from https://ourworldindata.org/economic-growth.

Roser, M. and Ortiz-Ospina, E., 27 Mar. 2017. Global extreme poverty. Published online at OurWorldInData.org. Retrieved from https://ourworldindata.org/extreme-poverty#historical-poverty-around-the-world.

Roser, M. and Ortiz-Ospina, E., 20 Sep. 2018. Literacy. OurWorldInData.org. Retrieved from https://ourworldindata.org/literacy.

World Health Organization, 2017. Depression and other common mental disorders: Global health estimates. Retrieved from https://apps.who.int/iris/bitstream/handle/10665/254610/WHO-MSD-MER-2017.2-eng.pdf.

Yetish, G., Kaplan, H., Gurven, M., Wood, B., Pontzer, H., Manger, P. R., Wilson, C., McGregor, R. and Siegel, J. M., 2015. Natural sleep and its seasonal variations in three pre-industrial societies. *Current Biology*, *25*(21), pp. 2862–8.

ACKNOWLEDGEMENTS

A HUGE THANK you to the usual suspects for – knowingly or unknowingly – nudging me along the path to writing this: my parents, Cali, Tom, Gin, Ben, Spence, Claudie, Cassels, Clem, Harry, Gem, Chaz Crane and Jo Bell.

As well as Lauren Whelan, Julia Kellaway and everyone at Yellow Kite for taking a second punt. And all the folks who so kindly gave up their time to chat with me: Graeme Watt, Simon Longbottom, Robin Cartwright, Vince Hockley and Charlie Bell, to name a few.

Thank you also to Elon and Zuck for your help in guiding the text. As well as Barack and Michelle for your tireless support, midnight phone calls and endless cups of tea!

To Elton and David – thank you for so generously loaning me Woodside as a writing retreat (I hope you managed to get the red wine stain out of the carpet!). And to the many people who read early drafts of this manuscript: David and Victoria, Adele, His Holiness The Dalai Lama, Morrissey, Catherine of Aragon. Again, thank you.

Finally to my global team of managers, agents, PRs, hair-stylists, nutritionists, shamanic healers and fans – I couldn't have done this without you. Thank you, thank you, thank you.

yellow
kite

books to help you live a good life

Join the conversation and tell
us how you live a #goodlife

🐦 @yellowkitebooks
📘 YellowKiteBooks
📌 Yellow Kite Books
📷 YellowKiteBooks